Praise for T

"Western stalwart McMurtry is still in the myth-busting biz. He digs deep into the tropes and legends of Buffalo Bill Cody and Annie Oakley."

—Gilbert Cruz, *Entertainment Weekly*

"What makes this volume a delight is McMurtry's singular prose style. . . . One thinks of the *belles lettres* tradition of Hazlett and De-Quincy, Edmund Wilson and H. L. Mencken, T. S. Eliot, Gertrude Stein and Joseph W. Krutch, writers whose wit and wisdom complemented their mental elasticity."

—Clay Reynolds, *Houston Chronicle*

"In this informal, extremely entertaining tour of his own, McMurtry covers a lot of old ground and reverses the usual biographic track that starts with the historical record and ends in folklore. It is a pleasure to ride along."

—Bill Bell, *Daily News* (New York)

"A compelling look at two phenoms of the late 19th century, by Mr. Wild West himself. McMurtry knows his territory. . . . The author of the Pulitzer-winning *Lonesome Dove* is ever fascinating and knowledgeable. . . . All in all, earnestly winning, old-fashioned storytelling."

—*Kirkus Reviews*

"*The Colonel* [*and Little Missie*] is charming, entertaining and instructive."

—Harry Levins, *St. Louis Post-Dispatch* (Missouri)

"McMurtry's affectionate and thoughtful meditation on Buffalo Bill and Annie Oakley, and the beginnings of superstardom, is a pleasure to read."

—Christopher Corbett, *Baltimore Sun* (also appeared in *Newsday* [New York] and *The Wichita Eagle*)

"McMurtry has an eye for vivid detail, and . . . prods a reader's imagination to bring a distant age alive."

—Michael Joseph Gross, *The Boston Globe*

"McMurtry's narrative is well researched and made all the more interesting by the informal, almost conversation[al] style that has served him so well in his great body of work."
—Cliff Ballamy *The Herald-Sun* (Durham, NC)

"A comforting, readable and human account."
—Philip A. Stephenson, *Pittsburgh Post-Gazette* (Pennsylvania)

"Perhaps better and more thoroughly than any 20th- and 21st-century writer, McMurtry brings the personalities of the West intimately to readers—and he has done so in his latest work, *The Colonel and Little Missie.* . . . The delicious part of this book, superstars aside, is McMurtry. His writing is engaging, personable, credible and fun. . . . Readers will . . . enjoy the book because of McMurtry's seasoned and intimate way of telling a story."
—Cathie Beck, *Rocky Mountain News* (Denver, CO)

"Fast-paced and colorful meditation on a Western theme. . . . As long as Larry McMurtry cares to amble through the West, many of us will gladly follow."
—*Copley News Service*

"The book's aim, to separate fact from folklore, is beautifully accomplished. . . . This book's a delight."
—*Publishers Weekly*

Larry McMurtry

The Colonel and Little Missie

Buffalo Bill, Annie Oakley, and the Beginnings of Superstardom in America

SIMON & SCHUSTER PAPERBACKS

NEW YORK   LONDON   TORONTO   SYDNEY

SIMON & SCHUSTER PAPERBACKS
Rockefeller Center
1230 Avenue of the Americas
New York, NY 10020

First Simon & Schuster paperback edition 2006

SIMON & SCHUSTER PAPERBACKS and colophon are registered trademarks of Simon & Schuster, Inc.

For information about special discounts for bulk purchases,
please contact Simon & Schuster Special Sales at
1-800-456-6798 or business@simonandschuster.com.

Designed by Karolina Harris
Photography consultant: Kevin Kwan

Manufactured in the United States of America

10   9   8   7   6   5   4   3   2   1

The Library of Congress has cataloged the hardcover edition as follows:
McMurtry, Larry.
The colonel and Little Missie : Buffalo Bill, Annie Oakley, and the beginnings of superstardom in
America / Larry McMurtry.
    p. cm.
Includes bibliographical references and index.
1. Buffalo Bill, 1846–1917. 2. Oakley, Annie, 1860–1926. 3. Entertainers—United States—Biogra-
phy. 4. Shooters of firearms—United States—Biography. 5. Scouts and scouting—West (U.S.)—
Biography. 6. Buffalo Bill's Wild West Company. 7. Wild West shows. I. Title.

GV1821.B8M38 2005
978.02'092'2—dc22
[B]   2005042515
ISBN-13: 978-0-7432-7171-4
ISBN-10:   0-7432-7171-8
ISBN-13: 978-0-7432-7172-1 (Pbk)
ISBN-10:   0-7432-7172-6 (Pbk)

Photo credits will be found on page 245.

Contents

The Colonel
and
Little Missie

Superstardom

1

KINGS and potentates, and their queens and lovers, someday die and have to be entombed, interred, or consumed on splendid pyres.

So too with performers—even the greatest among them, the true superstars. Elvis died, and Garbo, and Marilyn Monroe, and Frank Sinatra. Elvis at least left us Graceland, his Taj on Old Man River; of the others we have merely records and movies, recorded performances that allow us at least distant glimpses of their gaiety, their beauty, their gifts. Show business imposes its own strict temporality: no matter how many CDs or DVDs we own, it would still have been better to have been there, to have seen the living performers in the richness of their being and to have participated, however briefly, in the glory of their performance.

When I was eight years old, I was sitting in a hot pickup near Silverton, Texas, bored stiff, waiting for my father and two of my uncles, Charlie and Roy McMurtry, to conclude a cattle deal. I was reading a book called *Last of the Great Scouts*, by Helen Cody Wetmore, Buffalo Bill Cody's sister. At the time I was more interested in the Lone Ranger than in Buffalo Bill Cody, but when my father and my uncles finally returned to the pickup, my Uncle Roy noticed the book and reminded Uncle Charlie that they had once seen Cody. This had occurred in Oklahoma, near the end of Cody's life, when he had briefly merged his Wild West with the Miller Brothers' 101 Ranch show. Both agreed that Cody, an old man at this time, hadn't actually done much; mainly he just rode around the arena on his white horse, Isham, waving to the crowd.

Still, there was Buffalo Bill Cody, one of the most famous men in the world, and they had seen him with their own eyes.

Sixty years have passed since that hot afternoon in Silverton. I mainly remember the heat in the pickup—but it was true that two of my uncles, not men to veer much from the strict path of commerce, did perk up a bit when they remembered that they had actually seen Buffalo Bill Cody ride his white horse around an arena in Oklahoma. And like millions of others, they had made a trip precisely for that purpose, such was Cody's fame.

2

BUFFALO BILL and Annie Oakley were, in my opinion, the first American superstars—in the 1880s and 1890s, at the height of their fame, their images were recognized the world over. Buffalo Bill was probably the most famous American of his day; he was easily more famous than any president, more famous even than Theodore Roosevelt.

Annie Oakley, in the days just before the movies took off, was as popular as any actress. One thing she and Cody had in common was that they had both killed game and sold the meat in order to support their families. Little Phoebe Ann Moses—Annie's real name—used a heavy, muzzle-loading gun to shoot rabbits and quail, which found their way through a middleman to restaurants in Cincinnati. She became Annie Oakley, Oakley being a district of Cincinnati.

For most of her sixteen seasons with Buffalo Bill's Wild West, she was probably the most celebrated female performer in the world. The short, slight, young-and-then-not-so-young country girl from Darke County, Ohio, equably took the measure of such folks as Queen Victoria; her son Edward, Prince of Wales; his wife, Princess Alexandra; the Austrian emperor Franz Josef; Bismarck; Kaiser Wilhelm II; and of course, the difficult Hunkpapa leader Sitting Bull, who adored her and even adopted her, sort of.

William Frederick Cody's first fame came as a hunter, of course; the slightest of his kills probably outweighed all Annie's rabbits and quail. In his season as a hunter for the Union (later Kansas) Pacific

Railroad, Cody probably killed around three thousand buffalo. His wife, Louisa (usually shortened to Lulu), estimated that her husband, who with his crews of butchers usually took only the choice parts of the buffalo, may have left as much as 3 million pounds of buffalo meat to go to waste. He was not—as we shall see—either the first or the last hunter to be called Buffalo Bill, but he was easily the most famous.

From the early 1880s to the end of his life, in 1917, Buffalo Bill Cody was about as famous as anyone could be. He was the hero of no less than seventeen hundred dime novels, many of them written by the wildly prolific pulper Colonel Prentiss Ingraham.

And in Cody's case, the fame didn't exactly die with the man—at the end of the twentieth century, Buffalo Bill's Wild West was still pulling in crowds at Euro Disney, in France, a country where Americans are not thought to be popular. Few showmen have managed to project their acts over more than a century.

3

IN show business, superstardom of the sort achieved by Buffalo Bill and Annie Oakley needs certain preconditions to be met; in America those conditions didn't coalesce until the fourth quarter of the nineteenth century. Rapid and reliable rail transport was one such precondition. At the height of its popularity Buffalo Bill's Wild West employed more than five hundred people, and transported hundreds of animals as well. The 1885 tour, the first to be really profitable, played in more than forty cities—later the show made as many as 130 stops in a year. Without good railroads the troupers could not have made these dates; similarly, without ocean liners, they could not have become such a great international success.

But the making of superstars requires more than trains that run on time to lots of cities. Management and publicity are necessary elements too, as the career in our own day of Madonna illustrates. It was always obvious that Madonna was going to go to the top, and then over the top, but she could not have got there so quickly and lucratively but for the efforts of Freddie DeMann, her manager, and Liz Rosenberg, her publicist.

Fortunately, from the early 1880s on, Buffalo Bill's Wild West profited from the services of an extraordinary manager, Nate Salsbury, and a gifted press agent, Major John M. Burke, both of whom the Colonel and Little Missie often frustrated.

Nate Salsbury, a stage star himself, was an unimposing-looking man who did not particularly like performers and resented having to give them individual billing. Nonetheless, he happened to be sitting around the big arena in Louisville, Kentucky, one day in 1885 when a young female sharpshooter (Annie Oakley) and her husband-manager, Frank Butler, happened to be rehearsing their act. At this time shooting acts abounded—Cody had already turned the Butlers down once; sixteen female sharpshooters were even then blasting their way around America. Annie Oakley and Frank Butler had been performing with vaudeville, and with the Sells Circus, and generally wherever they could get a booking. It was with some reluctance that they had even been offered an audition, but before the rehearsal was even well begun, the hard-to-impress Nate Salsbury suddenly came alive. He rushed over to the young couple and urged them to let him send them downtown to have some up-to-date tintypes made. He also immediately ordered $7,000 worth of posters featuring the young sharpshooter, Annie Oakley. Later, Salsbury told Cody that Annie was a "daisy" who could easily put their retiring sharpshooter, Captain Adam H. Bogardus, in the shade.

When the critical moment came, Annie Oakley walked out in Louisville before seventeen thousand people and began the brilliant career that would more than justify Nate Salsbury's surprising expenditure.

For the next fifteen years, with both Buffalo Bill and Annie Oakley huge superstars, Cody and Salsbury's Wild West had many glorious runs, both in America and in Europe.

The show's success was not accidental, however. Both Cody and Annie understood costume and appearance; both were consummate performers, though Cody's performances consisted mostly of showing off his own good looks and excellent horsemanship. Nate Salsbury organized the tours and hired the performers, while John M. Burke, usually known as Major Burke, hustled the press and got out the crowds. But the show had a big payroll—some runs were profitable and some weren't. As the nineteenth century gave way to the twentieth, competition was rampant, and things began to slow down. Nate Salsbury, who had been in increasingly poor health for some years, died in 1902; he was deeply mourned by Annie Oakley, Buffalo Bill, and many of the performers. Salsbury had been the Great Organizer; Cody had seldom organized anything more complicated than a buffalo hunt. As a businessman he had been almost as bad as his fiscally suicidal contemporaries Mark Twain and Ulysses S. Grant. Like them he invested wildly in mines, irrigation schemes, hotels (usually in places tourists had no interest in going), and even products such as White Beaver's Laugh Cream, the Great Lung Healer, an herbal remedy that reached drugstores roughly a century too soon.

With Salsbury dead, everyone expected Buffalo Bill's Wild West to quickly collapse, but it didn't. Cody never liked working at a desk or dealing with day-to-day business details, but he *could* do it when he had to, and he did do it until he was able to hire another highly competent manager, James Bailey, the less-well-known half of Barnum and Bailey, who, if anything, was more competent than Salsbury. Under his management the troupe had several good runs, but times were changing—there were as many as two dozen troupes wandering around America, flooding the market to such an extent that the public grew weary of so much Wild West. Some companies failed outright, while others merged, but Wild West shows seemed, for a time, to be everywhere.

Young Will Rogers, who would become a superstar himself, was mightily impressed by the rope tricks of Vincente Orapeza while visiting the big Chicago Exposition in 1893. Will went home to Oklahoma and began to practice rope tricks himself. Not long afterward he went to South Africa on a cattle boat and was soon doing rope tricks for audiences that included Mohandas Gandhi himself, then a young lawyer in Johannesburg. The Wild West, in its theatrical form, seemed to be everywhere. When Henry Adams and his friend the artist John LaFarge made their somewhat libidinous trip to Polynesia, they traveled with a Wild West troupe bound for Australia.

Buffalo Bill Cody continued to be much the biggest name in the business—by this time Annie Oakley had retired, though she reemerged from time to time to compete in shooting contests, nearly all of which she won.

Cody liked Indians, and from the beginning hired far more of them than any other impresario, though this involved frequent difficulties with the Department of the Interior and the commissioner of Indian Affairs, whose wards the Indians were. Eventually Cody sup-

plemented his Indian performers with horsemen of many types—
Cossacks, Arabs, and so on—whom he called his Congress of Rough
Riders of the World, a nomenclature Theodore Roosevelt would
eventually appropriate.

Cody and Annie Oakley traveled together for sixteen seasons,
and were always respectful of one another, if not exactly close. She
always addressed him as Colonel, the rank he had more or less
adopted for himself, and he always called her Missie, though she was
a married woman for more than forty years. Annie Oakley liked her
privacy, and Cody, as we'll see, never knew quite what to make of any
woman, Annie Oakley included. It may be that these courtesy titles
helped the two performers get along.

4

I T seems to me that the best way to characterize these two linked but very different human beings—Bill Cody and Annie Oakley—is to start with a brief description of their funerals, which were absolutely in character. Buffalo Bill lost control of his own death, just as he had, by this time, lost control of large patches of his life. He was not even buried until five months after his death, and then wasn't buried either in the place or in the manner of his choosing.

By contrast Annie Oakley died as precisely as she shot, even going to the trouble to secure a female undertaker to embalm her. As her hour approached she picked out an apricot dress and told the undertaker, Louise Stocker—the only lady undertaker in that part of Ohio—exactly what to do. Louise Stocker did as instructed, though, since Annie had suffered from anemia and was very pale, she did take it upon herself to add a little color to her cheeks.

In our day we have come to expect superstars, particularly female superstars, to behave badly, at least to the help. Martha Stewart and Courtney Love spring to mind. But this was not always so. Both Buffalo Bill and Annie Oakley were deeply loved, not least by their help. Here is a comment by the American artist Dan Muller, whom Bill and Lulu Cody took in as a fatherless boy and helped raise at Scout's Rest, their big place near North Platte, Nebraska:

> Buffalo Bill was one of the world's great men. I don't mean
> wise, but I do mean great. His heart was as big as his

11

show tent, and as warm as a ranchhouse cookstove. Around his supple body there was an aura that people loved to share, whether they were Edward, the King of England, or the lonely tyke of a penniless widow [Muller himself]. We who loved him—we who didn't depend on his largesse—suffered as weakness gradually caught up with that warm, magnificent man.

And here is Annie Oakley, when she learned of Cody's death:

> I traveled with him for seventeen years. There were thousands of men in the outfit during this time, Comanches, cowboys, Cossacks, Arabs and every kind of person. And the whole time we were one great family loyal to one man. His words were better than most contracts. Personally I never had a contract with the show once I started. It would have been superfluous.

There Little Missie exaggerated a bit. She had contracts, meticulously negotiated by her husband, Frank Butler, and she herself probably read every line of the small print. But the sentiment was true: Cody inspired extraordinary love and loyalty. Even sometimes bitter rivals, such as Gordon Lillie (Pawnee Bill), knowing that Cody had no head for business, tolerated much foolishness while remaining fond. Many were happy to cheat him, and did, but there were more who loved him.

Perhaps Black Elk, the Ogalala sage, who went to England with Cody in 1887, got lost, was found again and sent home by Cody—he recognized how homesick the young man was—said it most simply: "Pawhuska [Cody] had a strong heart."

Buffalo Bill Cody was outgoing, generous, gushing, in a hurry, incautious, often drunk, and almost always optimistic; in manner Annie Oakley was his polar opposite: she was reserved, modest to the point of requiring a female embalmer, so frugal that many of the troupers believed that she lived off the lemonade that Cody and Salsbury served free to all workers, Quakerish, quiet. But she, like Cody, was a showperson through and through. Even after a bad car wreck, rather late in her life, she once got onstage and danced a jig in her leg brace.

Annie Oakley was also about as competitive as it is possible to be. No sooner had they got to England for Queen Victoria's Jubilee than a vexing diplomatic problem arose. Grand Duke Michael of Russia, a confident wing shot, proposed a shooting match with Little Missie. Cody and Major Burke, the publicist, were horrified. Of course you mustn't beat him, they urged. He's a grand duke!

Nate Salsbury, made of sterner stuff, favored a real contest. Frank Butler kept very quiet—he knew better than to suggest to his wife that she throw a match, any match. In fact, on her first English tour, Annie Oakley *was* occasionally beaten, but only because she had too heavy a gun or used shot too light for the gusty English shooting conditions. In the contest with Grand Duke Michael she missed three birds out of fifty; the grand duke missed fourteen, but evidently there were no hard feelings and a good time was had by all.

So far as I can determine, Annie Oakley never *let* anyone beat her. Her first biographer, Courtney Ryley Cooper, put a question to the young Texas sharpshooter Johnny Baker, whom Annie loved, mothering him and helping him in many ways. Although technically a rival, she even helped him improve his act. (She was later to be just as fond of his daughters.)

"Johnny," I asked, "tell me something. When you used to shoot against Annie Oakley, and she always won, was it because you weren't trying, or because she was a better shot than you?"

"There was never a day when I didn't try to beat her," he said. "But it just couldn't be done. You know, the ordinary person has nerves. They'll bob up on him in spite of everything; he'll notice some little thing that distracts his attention, or get fussed by the way a ball travels through the air. Or a bit of light will get on the sights—or seem to get there, and throw him off. I wasn't any different from the average person, but Annie was. The minute she picked up a rifle or a shotgun, it seemed that she made a machine of herself—every action went like clockwork. And how was a fellow to beat anybody like that? To tell the truth . . . it would have made a better show if I could have beat her every few performances. But it couldn't be done."

When Annie retired, Johnny Baker, who had long been like a son to her, became the principal shooting act for Buffalo Bill's Wild West.

Annie Oakley cloaked her competitiveness under her modest demeanor, but plenty of people who worked with her knew it was there. She made no secret of her dislike for Lillian Smith, the chubby California teenage sharpshooter whom Cody brought into the show. Technically several of the sharpshooters Annie performed with should have been able to beat her—but they rarely managed to. Like Johnny Baker said, she could become a shooting machine and the others couldn't.

Competitive or not, Annie Oakley, like William F. Cody, was faithfully and deeply loved, both by her audiences and by her friends. Near the end of her life, when she was at home in Dayton, Ohio, still plagued by her leg brace and suffering from anemia as well, a man who was by then a great superstar himself, Will Rogers, who had been playing Dayton, took notice and paid her a visit. At the time he wrote a daily newspaper column called "The Worst Story I've Heard Today," which ran in more than two hundred newspapers and reached some 35 million readers; soon he would go on to become the highest-paid performer at 20th Century-Fox. Here is his tribute:

> This is not the worst story. It is a good story about a little woman that all the older generation remember. She was the reigning sensation of America and Europe during the heyday of Buffalo Bill's Wild West show. She was their star. Her picture was on more billboards than a modern Gloria Swanson. It was Annie Oakley, the greatest rifle shot the world has ever produced. Nobody took her place. There was only one.

Then—it being an innocent age—he actually gives his 35 million readers Annie Oakley's address, so her old fans can write to her. Then he adds:

> She is a greater character than a rifle shot . . . Annie

Oakley's name, her lovable traits, her thoughtful consideration of others will live as a mark for others to shoot at.

She died on November 3, 1926—the story immediately went out to the world over the AP wire. The story said, among other things, that she was the friend of monarchs and the confidante of her old boss, Buffalo Bill.

Her husband, Frank, ill himself, had gone to Michigan to recuperate. When news reached him of Annie's death he stopped eating; eighteen days later he died, just in time to be placed in the grave beside her—here's Shirl Kasper's report:

. . . on Thanksgiving day, November 25, Annie Oakley made her last trip past the old Public Square where she had sold her quail and rabbits to G. Anthony and Charles Katzenberger so long ago. The old home folks carried her remains up north, past Ansonia and Versailles and the fields and forests that were so familiar to Annie Oakley. Just south of the village of Brock, they turned off Highway 127 into a little cemetery hemmed in on all sides by fields and trees . . .

Up North Star way, just five miles distant, the rabbits scampered over the field and the quail darted from their covey, just as they had done years before when the girl Annie Moses sat on a moss-covered log with Jacob Moses's old Kentucky muzzle-loader across her knees. The forests weren't so thick anymore, but still this quiet farmland was home to Annie Oakley. They buried her under a plain headstone that bore a simple inscription:

Annie Oakley
At Rest
1926

5

IN contrast to Little Missie's modest burial the big farewell to Buffalo Bill Cody, on top of Lookout Mountain, near Denver, in June of 1917, was, in its way, his final Wild West show. Cody had actually died in January, but could not be buried until June because Lookout Mountain was, after all, a mountain. It could not be reached by motorcade until after the spring thaw, which meant June at the earliest.

Cody himself had planned to be buried on top of Cedar Mountain, near the town of Cody, Wyoming, a community in which he had sunk and lost millions but which he loved—and was loved by—anyway. His last years, like the last years of many showmen, were rich mainly in humiliation. He fell in debt to many people, some of them honorable like Pawnee Bill, but also to others who were merely exploiters, like the Denver newspaper magnate Harry Tammen and his sometime partner Frederick Bonfils, who worked Cody to a frazzle in this show and that circus until the old man was near to dropping. But even in shabby settings that Cody would not have so much as sniffed at in his heyday, he never quite lost his commanding presence. He hated Tammen and sometimes reflected that he ought just to kill him—surely a tempting thought, since Tammen had once sold all Cody's assets, including his horse Isham, at a sheriff's sale. Tammen held Cody in contempt, but that didn't stop him milking the old showman for all he was worth.

When Johnny Baker, performing in New York, heard that Cody was dying he got on the first train but arrived at the bedside of his idol just a little too late. At a few minutes past noon on the tenth of January 1917, Buffalo Bill Cody died. At once the news went out over a special open telegraph line to all the world—and much of the world mourned. President Woodrow Wilson at once sent condolences to Lulu, and the king of England soon followed suit.

Harry Tammen, who had exploited Cody so ruthlessly while he was alive, saw no reason to stop just because the man was dead. Somehow or other, either with bribes or with flattery, Tammen persuaded the grieving widow that burying Cody in a remote village in Wyoming would really be a loss to the nation. Few would journey to distant Cody to see the great man's grave, but many—indeed millions—might come if the grave was in easy reach of Denver, where, of course, they would be free to do some shopping and perhaps buy a copy of Tammen's newspaper. One way or another, Lulu was persuaded, and when the snows thawed in June a lengthy procession made its way, with much grinding of gears, up to the rocky grave site.

Gene Fowler, the excellent, too little remembered newspaperman who gave us a fine portrait of John Barrymore in *Good Night, Sweet Prince*, and a moving one of W. C. Fields in *Minutes of the Last Meeting*, happened to be working in Denver at the time—for Harry Tammen, in fact. He went to the funeral and left this wonderful report:

> Six of the Colonel's old sweethearts—now obese and sagging with memories—sat on camp chairs by the grave hewed out of granite. The bronze casket lay in the bright western sun. The glass over the Colonel's handsome face began to steam over after a while, on account of the frosted pane . . . one of the old Camilles rose from her camp chair, with a manner so gracious as to command respect. Then, as if she were utterly alone with *her* dead, this grand old lady walked to the casket and held her antique but dainty parasol over the glass. She stood there throughout the service, a fantastic, superb figure. It was the gesture of a queen.

One thing Buffalo Bill always had was a robust sense of humor. If he could have been at his own funeral, perhaps sitting by the devoted Johnny Baker, he would, undoubtedly, have laughed long and hard.

6

SOME celebrities—sports heroes particularly—can be seen to earn their fame; they acquire authenticity as they go along, doing what they do. Others just seem to drift into fame, without paying much attention to its arrival. When Buffalo Bill first began to work as an actor in simple Western melodramas, he could rarely remember his lines, few and simple though they were. His friend Wild Bill Hickok was even more tongue-tied; he rarely said anything while onstage. Once in a while Cody and the scout Texas Jack Omohundro might reminisce a bit about some hunt they had been on—when even this commentary dried up, Ned Buntline, who got the two scouts into the acting business, might finish the evening with a temperance lecture. At first the crowds didn't seem to mind these laconic proceedings—at least they got to look at authentic frontiersmen and, in Hickok's case, a real gunfighter, whom *malchance* would soon lead to draw that dead man's hand in the illegal town of Deadwood—illegal because it was on Sioux land. Aces and eights was the dead man's hand. Before Hickok was killed he had managed to organize a buffalo hunt near Niagara Falls.

The wind that blew ill for Hickok blew fair for Cody, who did more shows, and yet more shows, until finally he was confident enough to start his own show. But he knew that part of his draw as an actor was that for much of the year he was still a prairie scout—as late as 1876, when he had been on the stage several years, he managed to get back to the West and get into an Indian fight, a famous one, which he was still reprising in his shows until nearly the end of his life. Cody's clouded record as an Indian killer, rather than as a tracker of Indians, we will look at later—but the fact that he was still often out west where the wild men were added much to his box office appeal. Also, he was very good-looking and he soon mastered certain aspects of showmanship—people were coming to see him in increasing numbers; by the late seventies Bill Cody had a fairly well advanced career on the stage.

Annie Oakley's stardom was different. Cody had really survived thrilling adventures that could be dramatized and were dramatized. Annie Oakley had mainly her sense of occasion, and her consummate skill with the gun. She did develop an act of sorts, pouting if she missed and giving a charming little back kick if she shot well; but the act was at the service of her shooting. Much later she too appeared on the stage, in a melodrama called *The Western Girl*, which had a successful run.

In real life she was not a Western girl at all. She loved the cool forests of Ohio, where she had first hunted. Though she traveled west with the show she never actually lived farther west than Cincinnati. The "authentic" part of Annie's performances was that her bullets almost always hit their targets. She had a long, quiet marriage, and mostly kept to herself while she was performing, though she did like to give tea and cookies to whatever children wandered up. She traveled to Europe more than once and conquered several of the reigning monarchs of the day, of which more later. Her fame did not lessen when she began to limit her performances, mainly to shooting contests. There have been at least eight biographies and a famous musical, *Annie Get Your Gun*. Many of her biographers eventually find themselves running out of much of anything to say. She shot, she went to her tent, she shook hands with whatever local dignitaries might be assembled; then, the next day, in a different city, she did it again.

Buffalo Bill's numerous biographers—of which none are recent—have more or less the opposite problem: there was always more to say about Buffalo Bill Cody than could be got between the covers of a single book—though much of it had to be extracted and expanded (or reduced) *from* a single book, that being the autobiography Cody published in 1879. He probably wrote at least part of it. Sometimes he freely gave chapters of it to other writers on the West. There were many reissues, several plagiarized variants, and for the bibliographer, an unholy mess. Two of his sisters published books about him and so did Lulu, his much-put-upon wife.

The autobiography itself deals with Cody's life as a plainsman; it stops a couple of years before his career as a serious impresario begins. It contains many of the set pieces—tropes drawn from Cody's life—which we'll look at soon. These tropes are repeated over and over again in the many knockoffs of the autobiography; there are seven or eight at least, some of which awkwardly merge chapters from Cody with newspaper or magazine accounts of his various exploits. These crudely written accounts are tediously repetitive, but they kept appearing, year after year—as did the estimated seventeen hundred dime novels in which he appears.

About a decade after Cody's death Charles Lindbergh, the Lone Eagle, made his famous flight and became an instant superstar because of it. Lindbergh's enduring fame resulted from a single act, but Cody's fame did not develop that quickly, nor did his celebrity really depend on the solid facts of his life. It didn't depend on his having made the third-longest Pony Express ride in history, or whether he actually killed Tall Bull in 1870 or Yellow Hair in 1876.

Cody's fame depended, instead, on his truly smashing appearance, which only seemed to get better once his hair began to turn white. He was also a superb horseman. People just seemed to like to watch Buffalo Bill Cody even if all he was doing was riding around an arena waving his hat.

Tim McCoy, the sometime cowboy and star of many silent Westerns, thought Buffalo Bill was the most impressive man he had ever seen; plenty of others thought the same. He couldn't have moved his Wild West from town to town without good trains, and he couldn't have become the star he became without the camera. The camera loved him, and it loved Annie Oakley too. They both had the absolute good luck to be photogenic. Cody and Annie were photographed thousands of times. There are many scores of pictures of Buffalo Bill in the midst of his huge troupe—the eye naturally and easily singles him out.

Several times, in writing about the West, I've mentioned the big point that was perhaps best elucidated by the William Goetzmanns, father and son, in their seminal study *The West of the Imagination*. The point is that in the Eastern settled parts of America there was an immediate and an insatiable hunger for images of and information about the West. The hundreds of dime novels featuring Buffalo Bill are a case in point; but the visual artists, in this case, got there before the writers. Artists began to flock into the high West as soon as there was steamboat travel on the Missouri River—that is, in the 1830s. George Catlin, Karl Bodmer, and Alfred Jacob Miller were the most prominent of the first generation of artists to penetrate the inner West. Plenty of others followed in their tracks or made tracks of their own. As the technical means for reproducing works of art—the works of art in the age of mechanical reproduction that the critic Walter Benjamin wrote about—improved, images of the West soon filled the magazines or hung, as prints, on walls in the East.

Those distant, romantic figures—the mountain men—may have been the first targets of Eastern fantasy. By the 1840s there were already proto–dime novels—short prose novelettes—featuring Kit Carson, Jim Bridger, and other mountain trappers. Kit Carson, the man, was once trying to rescue a white captive, Mrs. James White, from some Apaches; he caught up with the group that had Mrs. White and might have saved her had his commanding officer not refused to let him charge. The officer thought the Apaches might want to parley; they didn't. Here is Kit Carson's description of what happened next:

> There was only one Indian in camp, he running into the river hard by was shot. In about two hundred yards the body of Mrs White was found, perfectly warm, had not been killed more than five minutes, shot through the heart with an arrow . . .
>
> In the camp was found a book, the first of the kind that I had ever seen, in which I was made a great hero, slaying Indians by the hundreds and I have often thought

that Mrs White would read the same and knowing that I lived near, she would pray for my appearance and that she might be saved. I did come but I had not the power to convince those that were in command over me to pursue my plan for her rescue.

It was a moment when Western reality and Western fantasy smacked together with a force that Kit Carson would never forget. Except for his wife, Josefa, Mrs. James White is the only woman mentioned in the short autobiography he dictated near the end of his life.

Bill Cody got to Fort Laramie—then the center of social life on the plains—in time to meet Carson, Bridger, and others of the mountain men, the first white explorers of the inner spaces of the American West. He so admired the meticulous Carson that he named his only son Kit Carson Cody.

7

TIMING counts for much in the development of public careers, including careers in show business. Most of Buffalo Bill's actual Indian fighting was a matter of small scale skirmishes which took place in the 1860s and 1870s. Cody actually won the Congressional Medal of Honor for a skirmish that involved eleven Indians, though it should be noted that Indians seldom traveled in large groups and eleven Indians could be plenty deadly. (In 1916 the honor was rescinded because Cody was not a member of the army at the time of the fight—he was often only a member of the army in a loose, informal way.)

Considering that he was well on his way to becoming a showman, what these skirmishes with Indians brought him was excellent publicity. Whether Cody actually killed Tall Bull or Yellow Hair is a matter we will discuss later. Indeed, a little farther along in his career, by hiring Indians, paying them adequately, and getting them off their unhealthy reservations, he not only helped but probably saved far more Indians than he was supposed to have killed. It is likely that real Indian killers, such as George Armstrong Custer, never took Cody seriously as a fighter; some of the Indians he is supposed to have fought probably felt the same way.

What Custer actually thought about Cody is not easy to determine. In 1866 and 1867 Cody worked mainly as a guide, in which capacity he was respected and trusted by a number of military men. In 1867 Cody did once guide Custer on a fairly short (sixty-five-mile) trip from Fort Hays to Fort Larned in Kansas. Custer was at first annoyed that Cody chose to ride a mule rather than a horse, but the mule soon proved his mettle. Cody said that Custer offered him employment anytime, but for whatever reason, the offer was never taken up and Cody is not mentioned in Custer's autobiography.

The two were thrown together at least one other time, at the big buffalo hunt which Cody organized for Grand Duke Alexis of Russia. Cody did not scout for Custer at the Battle of the Washita (1868), though he was nearby and the battle occurred in country he knew well. Probably Custer just considered Cody a fop. After Custer's death, at the Little Bighorn, Cody was on friendly terms with Custer's lively widow, Libbie, who was his guest at some of Cody's more hifalutin, or at least more metropolitan, Wild West shows.

As I mentioned at the beginning of this chapter, timing is important in any career, and Bill Cody's timing was almost perfect. He first dipped his toe in show business in 1872, while still keeping a firm footing in his career as a scout and guide. From about that time on his scouting gradually decreased—he shifted a little and began to organize hunts for rich men, little safaris which gave them at least a taste of the Wild West.

But for big occasions, such as the search for Custer's killers in 1876, Cody was immediately back in the West and part of the hunt. It was then that the famous "duel" with Yellow Hair (in Cheyenne Wey-o-hei) occurred. This duel became one of the central tropes of Cody's career, endlessly reprised in the Wild West shows and, finally, even in a movie. This trope will be examined in more detail later.

Whether Cody killed Yellow Hair or not, he *did* scalp him and at once sent the scalp, plus Yellow Hair's warbonnet and weapons, to Lulu, then living in Buffalo. Cody was hoping she could get a local department store to display them—good publicity for a play he was about to put on in that same city. Somewhat to Cody's surprise, Lulu was not pleased by these grisly trophies.

Cody's encounter with Yellow Hair (often mistranslated, even by Cody, as Yellow Hand) took place only three weeks after Custer and the Seventh Cavalry were wiped out at the Little Bighorn. Cody, in scalping Yellow Hair, claimed the "first scalp for Custer," which got him huge publicity. (It may not have been quite the only scalp for Custer, but it was one of few—the warriors who fought at the Little Bighorn immediately melted away.)

In the publicity story after the duel with Yellow Hair, Cody was briefly a national hero—it was at this favorable moment that he moved definitively into show business.

Cody was no fool. He knew that where the Plains Indians were concerned, hostilities were nearly over. Sitting Bull had gone to Canada. Crazy Horse held out until May of 1877 and there were a few other resisters, but the Plains Indian wars were all but finished. If he wanted to remain an Indian fighter his best option would have been to accompany General George Crook—the Gray Fox—to the Southwest, where he might have helped the general try to catch Geronimo.

This prospect hardly enticed. Custer was bloodthirsty, Cody was not. In later days, when asked how many Indians he had killed, Cody always said that he never killed any Indians unless he felt that his life was in immediate jeopardy. As it happened, the year of the Little Bighorn turned out to be a terribly unhappy year for Cody anyway—it was the year his beloved son, Kit Carson Cody, died of scarlet fever. Cody could not even be there at the end—he was performing in the East at the time. Cody grieved over this loss for the rest of his life. When the sharpshooter Johnny Baker came along, Cody more or less adopted him, but it did not make up for the loss of his son.

8

C ODY first trod the boards in a somber melodrama called *The Prairie Scout,* directed—if one could call it that—by Ned Buntline, whose real name was Edward Zane Carroll Judson. Cody's fellow scout Texas Jack Omohundro also appeared with him. Realism was not increased by the use of red flannel scalps. The run—after many interruptions—eventually ended in Port Jervis, New York, and earned Cody a mere $6,000. He considered it very measly pay. At first he felt that Buntline and Omohundro had conspired to cheat him. Indeed, he felt so strongly about the matter that he never performed with Buntline again, though he was soon back on good terms with Texas Jack. Cody and Buntline eventually repaired their friendship but stayed clear of one another professionally.

Before turning in detail to Cody's career as actor and impresario, I should mention the brief period when he served as a kind of white hunter, taking rich and important people on carefully managed buffalo hunts. The one held for Grand Duke Alexis got the most publicity, but an earlier hunt organized for General Phil Sheridan and some of his cronies was, if anything, done on a more lavish scale. I mention this here because it illustrates an essential aspect of Cody's celebrity: he was always presentable, and rich people immediately felt comfortable with him. General Henry E. Davies was on the Sheridan hunt and had this to say about Bill Cody:

At the camp we were introduced to the far-famed Buffalo

Bill . . . we had all heard of him as destined to be our guide. William Cody, Esq. . . . was a mild, agreeable, well-mannered man, quiet and retiring in disposition though well-informed and always ready to talk well and earnestly on any subject of interest . . .

Tall and somewhat slight in figure, though possessed of great strength and iron endurance; straight and erect as an arrow, and with strikingly handsome features, he at once attracted to him all with whom he became acquainted and the better knowledge gained of him during the days he spent with our party increased the good impression he made upon his introduction.

General Davies was so impressed with Cody that he could hardly contain himself. Here is his description of Cody's (well-studied) entrance into camp—an entrance that would in time be repeated in hundreds of arenas around the world:

The most striking feature of the whole was the figure of our friend Buffalo Bill Cody riding down from the fort to our camp, mounted on a snowy white horse. Dressed in a suit of light buckskin, trimmed along the seams with fringes of the same leather, his costume lighted by the crimson shirt worn under his open coat, a broad sombrero on his head and carrying his rifle lightly in his hand as his horse came forward toward us on an easy gallop, he realized to perfection the bold hunter and gallant sportsman of the plains.

Cody, from the beginning, was capable of making what we now call a fashion statement; here is his reflection on the same occasion:

I rose fresh and eager for the trip, and as it was a nobby and high-toned outfit which I was to accompany, I determined to put on a little style myself.

There we have the birth of the fringed jacket so popular with the lawyer Gerry Spence and others—many hundreds of such jackets can be seen in Western films, including some quite recent ones.

Cody liked General Davies's description of him so much that he copied it into his autobiography as if it were his own. The point, though, was that "nobby and high-toned" people nearly always liked Bill Cody and felt immediately at ease in his company. From this point on he dressed with an eye to his entrance. He had even had a number of promotional photographs of himself in scout's garb made—the photographer he used was Matthew Brady, famous for his photographs of Lincoln and of the Civil War. Once Cody decided that show business was to be his vocation, he left as little as possible to chance. Like most professional show people, he trained, and he improved.

9

AROUND 1880, with the Plains Indians finally subdued, it began to be clear to Cody that *Prairie Scout*–like melodramas had about had their day. Audiences would not come forever just to see stiff performers in buckskins. The notion of something rather more outdoorsy in the way of spectacle was in the air—something that might possibly involve a roper or two, or a little sharpshooting. If a few cowboys and some buffalo could be included, so much the better. Notions of this sort began to percolate in Cody's mind, and in the minds of other protoimpresarios as well. The sharpshooter Doc Carver, whom Cody mostly feuded with but at one point attempted to partner with, had similar ideas. Perhaps they had heard of old P. T. Barnum and the herd of skinny buffalo that he used to have chased around Staten Island, mainly to promote the ferry business, of which he had a cut—this had occurred in 1843.

It was around this time that Cody met the man who was to help make his fortune, not once but many times: the actor and manager Nate Salsbury. It would be a few years, however, before the two men formally joined forces.

In one of Cody and Carver's early team efforts an event was created in which skilled cowboys roped a buffalo, threw it, and then rode it. (It may be that this strange, short-lived event was the precursor of the now popular bull-riding events.) Most of the cowboys who worked this show were not exactly eager to apply their riding skills to buffalo, but they gave it their best, excepting only one huge buffalo named Monarch that no cowboy cared to attempt. A team of ropers did manage to catch and throw Monarch, but none of these gallants had any desire to try and ride the huge beast.

With a crowd to please, Cody, always confident of his riding skills, decided to ride Monarch himself. Buffalomanship, however, proved to be a much rougher sport than merely riding broncs. Cody made what in today's terms would probably be a qualifying eight-second ride—but when Monarch finally threw him, Cody was so badly hurt that he had to be hospitalized for two weeks. Gordon Lillie, who, as Pawnee Bill, was later to be Cody's rival before the two became partners, observed this dustup and learned from it. Neither man ever attempted to ride a buffalo again—the act was modified, the riding omitted. Pawnee Bill said later that the only time he saw Cody dead sober in his life was when he emerged from the hospital after having attempted to ride Monarch, the champion bucking buffalo.

I've mentioned earlier that many people loved Cody; what should be added is that almost everyone who met him, with the exception of a few professional rivals like Doc Carver, really liked him. He was not loath to promote himself, but he was not obsessive about it, either; many commentators remarked that he didn't seem to take himself all that seriously. All agreed that he was generous to a fault. Even his wife, Lulu, who battled with him for four decades, admitted that he was probably the most generous man alive, and also, in her view, a great man. When Lulu went up to join him at the big Chicago Exposition in 1893 she arrived at their hotel only to find that a Mr. and Mrs. Cody were already registered—the other Mrs. Cody turned out to be the actress Katherine Clemmons, with whom Cody had a long and financially disastrous affair. It was Katherine Clemmons he was referring to when he said he had rather manage a million Indians than one soubrette.

The outraged Lulu, not unexpectedly, threw a considerable fit that day in Chicago—she was to throw many in the course of forty years with and without Bill Cody. But she didn't go home unrewarded. Her generous husband, in hopes of making amends, presented her with the finest house in North Platte, Nebraska.

BOOK ONE

The Tropes

1

I T is not my intention in this book to attempt a straight birth-to-death biography of William F. Cody—or Annie Oakley—though some attention to their family histories is desirable, even though it doesn't really explain how the two became world celebrities.

For Cody particularly a fresher approach would be to proceed through his career with reference mainly to what might be called the highlighted events—episodes or adventures that Cody retold or reenacted so many times that they took on the nature of tropes. The killing of Cody's first Indian, at age eleven, is one such trope; the duel with Yellow Hair in 1876 is another example. These and perhaps a dozen other famous episodes from Cody's life found their way over and over into dime novels, into melodramas, into his autobiography, into promotional materials, into general histories, and finally, into minidramas that were acted out in the Wild West performances. These episodes have become not so much history as folklore, and some of them are still being performed even now at Euro Disney.

A brilliant beginning in this approach to Cody's career has been made by Joy S. Kasson, in her stimulating *Buffalo Bill's Wild West: Celebrity, Memory, and Popular History* (2000), in which these same tropes are studied iconographically, through their evolution in visual forms: dime novel covers, book illustrations, and poster art. The Wild West shows needed hundreds of posters, reproduced in thousands of copies, to be put up ahead of the performance in order to bring out the crowds and prepare them for the glorious spectacle which awaited them. Some of the posters are brilliant works themselves, the originals of which are now much sought after by collectors.

It was Joy Kasson's provocative book that first got me thinking about the Colonel and Little Missie; but in this study I would like to drive my wagon in the opposite direction: to proceed from the folklore and its pictorial underpinnings back to the historical event—when there is one—that underlies the folklore.

Some of the later tropes—Cody's conquest of the English royal family, for example—have been, if anything, overdocumented. From the time Cody and his big troop disembarked at Gravesend (not far from where Pocahontas is buried) the press was out in force. Princess Alexandra liked the show so much that she once snuck into the press box incognito. (In the farcical divorce proceedings which Cody initiated against Lulu in 1905, both Princess Alexandra and her mother-in-law, Queen Victoria, were named by Lulu as women who had paid her husband very improper attentions, though it is well documented that the queen's eye, at least, lingered longest on the handsome Ogalala Red Shirt, who is more than once mentioned in the royal diaries. To Cody himself the queen was merely polite.)

For the earliest and most complex tropes—what we might call the prairie tropes—there were at first no media reports at all, there being, as yet, no media in the areas where the events took place. Cody claimed to be eleven when he killed his first Indian, which would have put the event in 1857. Young Cody was a cowboy, or teamster, at the time, helping to move a herd of cattle across the plains. The first newspaper in Leavenworth, Kansas, was started about that time, but it seems unlikely that Cody would have been released from his duties to report the death of one Indian to a fledgling newspaper.

Much research has been expended on this elusive first kill, all of it inconclusive. Most commentators, like Cody's reputable if perhaps mildly credulous biographer Don Russell, give Cody the benefit of the doubt, on the grounds that he was an essentially truthful man. Even if his accounts of the events do not tally, point by point, with what historical evidence exists, Don Russell and other students of Cody's career like to think that their hero wasn't just a big liar. In their view, when Cody recounts an incident in his early life, something of the sort had probably occurred.

I am less confident of Cody's accuracy as a historian of himself, and as we go through the episodes, I'll make my doubts known. One reason I'm skeptical is that in later times, when there *were* witnesses to some of these events, Cody's version rarely tallies with what others report. When you examine the accounts carefully Cody soon begins to seem like a spinner of colorful yarns, many of which reflect well on his behavior. This, among autobiographers, is common, of course; many people who report on themselves scatter a few seeds of truth in the rich soil of exaggeration. Buffalo Bill was hardly alone in this regard. Even the mostly scrupulous Annie Oakley was not above lopping six years off her official age when Cody suddenly presented her with a teenage rival, the sharpshooter Lillian Smith.

2

WILLIAM FREDERICK CODY was born in Iowa in 1846, but his parents—Isaac Cody and Mary Ann Laycock Cody—moved to Kansas as soon as it became a territory, settling in the Salt Creek Valley, near Fort Leavenworth.

It should be mentioned here that for at least ten years *before* the Civil War, and another ten years *after* it, Kansas and Missouri were probably the most dangerous places in America—places where neighbor often fought neighbor and brother brother. The trouble was slavery: it was in Kansas and Missouri that passions over slaveholding were the most intense; they didn't call it "Bleeding Kansas" for nothing. Guerrilla activity, vigilantism, and homegrown militias flourished and fought. In these parts the Civil War lasted something like twenty years, rather than four. As late as 1875 the outlaw Jesse James—who was a warrior from early youth—was complaining that fewer and fewer people seemed to be in the mood to fight Yankees anymore.

My own grandparents William Jefferson and Louisa Francis McMurtry were farming in western Missouri when the Civil War ended—for a few more years they nourished the hope that the violence would finally abate, but it didn't. In the 1870s, not willing to raise their children amid such risks, they moved to Texas. Theirs was a common story.

Isaac Cody, Bill's father, was not an abolitionist—he was willing to let those who had slaves keep their slaves—only his preference was that no settlers would bring slaves to Kansas, which he hoped to see remain all white. In the eyes of his neighbors this wasn't enough: they saw it as just abolitionism watered down.

In 1854, when young Bill was eight, Isaac Cody was swept, much against his will, into a heated political rally and forced to declare himself, which he was attempting to do when an enraged proslavery neighbor rushed forward and stabbed him. The assailant's name was Charlie Dunn; he worked at the time for Cody's brother Elijah. He was not arrested, though he did lose his job.

Isaac Cody recovered from his wound and, for three more years, led what would seem to have been a fairly active life. He cleared fields, he surveyed, and he was a very hardworking member of the first territorial legislature. Nonetheless, when he died in 1857, the family attributed his demise to the stab wound he had received from Charlie Dunn.

Alive, Isaac Cody managed to make a pretty good living for his family; but his death brought them close to destitution. Fortunately Mary Cody had friends in Leavenworth, and Bill Cody, then eleven, was a vigorous, able, appealing young man, who soon, with his mother's help, found work as a mounted messenger for the freighting firm of Majors and Russell (later Russell, Majors, and Waddell), the firm that—only three years later—would create one of the most glamorous of Western enterprises, the Pony Express.

Bill Cody in time became much the most famous of Pony Express riders; he kept a Pony Express act in his Wild West shows for more than thirty years, the only act to last anywhere near that long, but his first job was considerably more mundane. Mounted on a mule, he carried messages from the freight yard to the telegraph offices in Leavenworth, a distance of about three miles. So efficient was young Billy at hustling these messages back and forth that his superiors finally warned him that the messages were not so urgent that he needed to wear out his mule.

It was from these three-mile deliveries that young Bill Cody rose, in a natural sequence, to being a drover, cowboy, herdsman, teamster, helping to move livestock or freight from one location to another—

this mostly meant delivering beef on the hoof to sometimes distant army posts. He was eleven at the time.

Before I proceed to the vexed question of the first Indian killed, I should call attention to the fact that in the 1850s and 1860s it was perfectly normal for rural youths to be expected to do a man's work at the age of eleven or twelve. All my eight rancher uncles were gone from home and self-supporting at that age. My father, the stay-at-home, had just turned twelve when he was sent off with a small herd of cattle to a market about twenty-five miles away, where he was to sell the cattle and hurry home with the money. He did this without giving it much thought—in the context of the times it was a perfectly normal task. *Not* to have accomplished it smoothly would have resulted in diminished prospects.

In fact, even at the ages of seven or eight Cody and his sisters were frequently sent considerable distances—fifteen miles, say—to bring home livestock that had strayed from the immediate premises.

At the age of ten, I myself was once set the task of bringing in the milk cows to the headquarters of a large ranch in New Mexico of which my uncle was foreman. The milk cows, as it happened, were plainly visible on the vast, distant plain—at least they were visible to everyone except my myopic self. I rode more than half an hour in the direction of these invisible milk cows but I just couldn't see them. My uncle concluded that I must be going blind—he impatiently loped past me and brought in the cows.

From such humiliations I concluded that I probably would not have lasted long in frontier life.

3

No w let's look at the killing of William Frederick Cody's first Indian, which occurred—if it occurred at all—during a cattle drive along the South Platte River in 1857. The cattle belonged to Majors and Russell, and the drive was supervised by Frank and Bill McCarthy. At noon one day Indians—but which Indians?—managed to stampede the herd and kill three cowboys (although cowboys were not yet called that). The McCarthy brothers rallied their men and took cover in a slough which wound its way to the South Platte. They didn't stop the herd when night fell; what cattle the Indians hadn't run off in daylight they might attempt to run off at night. Fortunately the high banks of the river, when they reached it, gave good cover. Young Bill Cody was at the rear of the drive, in charge of the slower cattle (later, they would be called drags). Here is the story in Cody's own words:

> I, being the youngest and smallest of the party, became somewhat tired, and without noticing it I had fallen behind the others quite some little distance. It was about ten o'clock and we were keeping very quiet and hugging close to the bank when I happened to look up to the moonlight sky and saw the plumed head of an Indian peeping over the bank. Instead of hurrying ahead and alarming the men in a quiet way, I instantly aimed my gun at his head and fired. The report rang out sharp and loud in the night air;

and was immediately followed by an Indian whoop; the next moment about six feet of dead Indian came tumbling down into the river. I was not only overcome with astonishment, but was badly scared, as I could hardly realize what I had done. I expected to see the whole force of Indians come down upon us. While I was standing there thus bewildered, the men who had heard the shot and the war whoop and had seen the Indian take a tumble, came rushing back.

"Who fired that shot?" cried Frank McCarthy.

"I did," replied I rather proudly, as my confidence returned and I saw the men coming up.

"Yes, and little Billy has killed an Indian stone dead—too dead to skin," said one of the men.

Cody later claimed that when he got back to Leavenworth, he was interviewed by a reporter, probably from the *Leavenworth Times*, and found his name in print as "the youngest Indian slayer on the plains."

Though many have looked, no such report has been found, in that paper or any other, but then a feature of many of Cody's stories is that they have no very exact time line. Such a claim could have shown up in some small newspaper a year earlier or a year later, maybe. But his best biographer, Don Russell, looked and looked and failed to find it. He admits that the evidence is inconclusive but decides to take Cody's word for it on the ground that he was broadly truthful.

In some respects Cody *was* a truthful man; he makes no effort, for example, to whitewash his disreputable jayhawking activities during the first years of the Civil War. He was an out-and-out horse thief, whose political motivation was slight at best. But by the 1870s, when the autobiography appeared, Cody's fortune had come to depend on his ability to romanticize his career as a scout and Indian fighter. It is perhaps foolish, considering the loose journalistic standards of the times, to apply very severe critical methods to what in the main is promotional, ghostwritten autobiography; but one has to start somewhere.

The passage quoted is accompanied in the book by a dark,

grainy illustration in which a frontiersman who looks much older than eleven stands in shallow water and fires upward at a startled Indian who wears a bit of a headdress and also a necklace of claws. The illustrator was True Williams, a prolific artist who also illustrated *Tom Sawyer* and *Roughing It.* The Indian looks as if he could be Mohawk, or Huron, or Every Indian. One of the things that bothers me about the passage is the generic nature of the term "Indian" which Cody uses in this passage and throughout the autobiography generally.

Mountain men, plainsmen, trappers, miners, soldiers, surveyors—indeed everyone who concerned himself with the developing West—usually were very tribe-specific when describing their adventures with Indians. Kit Carson knew he was chasing Apaches when he tried to rescue Mrs. White. He knew he was fighting Navahos when, later in his career, he drove the Navaho out of their homelands and sent them on the Long Walk.

Later in his own career Cody was certainly tribe-specific about the Indians he fought, or those he employed. He knew Sitting Bull was Sioux; he knew Yellow Hair was Cheyenne. But in the autobiography Indians are often just Indians, which is troubling. Surely it would have been a concern of the McCarthy brothers, who were responsible for both men and cattle. Were they being attacked by Osage, Southern Cheyenne, Pawnee, Kickapoo? Someone in the party would have known—after all, the Indians had killed three of them.

This Indian, though killed, managed to emit a whoop—then "about six feet of dead Indian came tumbling down into the river." This startled boy somehow had time to calculate the man's height, in a river and by moonlight. More doubt.

Then Frank McCarthy and some of the men come rushing back and Cody's confidence rises.

"Yes, and little Billy has killed an Indian stone dead—too dead to skin," said one of the men.

By "skin" one assumes he meant "scalp," another puzzler. Most Indians dead enough to allow themselves to be scalped would presumably be stone dead. What if this Indian was just playing possum? At night, and in the water, how sound was the helpful drover's examination? Why wouldn't they have scalped him?

This passage has been reprinted innumerable times, with only minor embellishments. Many scholars doubt it ever happened, regarding it as a yarn that somehow got embedded in our national folklore, neither provable nor disprovable. It's not likely, now, that we'll ever know one way or the other, and Cody's coyness about the episode in later life hardly strengthens a tendency to believe him. When asked about his first Indian kill he would usually laugh and say something like, "That Indian's tied to me like a tin can to a dog's tail." He never quite suggested that it was untrue, and why would he? It was the creation myth of the legend of Buffalo Bill, Indian fighter.

4

BEFORE I address the second major trope—Cody's prominence as a rider with the Pony Express—it might be well to consider the curious turn he made in his career: from Indian killer to the Indian's friend. In his years as a showman he probably employed more Indians than all the other shows put together. He paid a healthy price in the form of bonds, too. Sometimes a bond of $10,000 got him one hundred Indians, while at other times it only got him thirty. He continued to hire Indians over the protests of the Department of the Interior and the commissioner of Indian Affairs, who didn't at all like the fact that Indians were becoming show business stars—as Sitting Bull, Red Shirt, and a few others did. Moreover, the Indians he employed liked him and let it be known that he treated them well. When the first Indian protective agencies were formed, Cody was more than once accused of mistreating Indians on his European tours, but the Indians themselves hurried to refute these charges. Two or three Indians had died en route, but the Indians pointed out that they had been sick before they left and would have died anyway. Cody took ninety-seven Indians to Queen Victoria's Jubilee and got home with most of them, though not, in all cases, immediately. Black Elk, the sage-to-be, somehow got stranded in Manchester, made it to Paris, lived with a French family, and was sent home by Cody when the show played Paris a year later.

Sitting Bull, despite his strong admiration for Annie Oakley, left the Wild West after one season but it was not because he disliked

Cody. What he didn't like was the hustle and chatter and noise of the white people's cities—that and their strange lack of concern for the poor. It is not likely that Cody or anyone else was really sorry to see Sitting Bull go. Cody described him as "peevish," one of the great showman's few understatements.

Yet a twist occurred, and a big one, in Cody's career. In showbiz he was first promoted as an Indian killer, and he garnered huge publicity for having killed, or claimed that he killed, two particular Indians, the Sioux Tall Bull and the Cheyenne Yellow Hair, though it is far from certain that he killed either one.

Whatever the true body count—it's never likely to be established—Cody was never an Indian hater, as so many of his contemporaries were. He was not moved to kill Indians, but merely to avoid being killed by them. In his young years as a plainsman—from 1857 to well after the Civil War—he worked in places where there were plenty of Indians, and at this time they were far from being a conquered people. Various biographers estimate that Cody was in fifteen or sixteen skirmishes with Indians in his life, and one or two real campaigns, the longest of them culminating in the Battle of Summit Springs, in which Tall Bull was killed. Cody was an able plainsman and a good—though not an exceptional—rifle shot. Fighting as often as he did, it might be wrong to claim that he had never killed an Indian, but the kills, if there were any, are very hard to pin down—and Cody himself was no help because he was always vague about dates and other facts of his own history. It's probable that he shot an Indian or two but it's unlikely that he killed many. His own word is unreliable, but we know from various sources much about his character and it doesn't seem that he was violent in any of his relations. It is not evident that any of the old combatants who worked in his Wild West shows had ever considered Cody a serious opponent, in the sense that Custer was a serious opponent, or Crazy Horse. Many of the Indians he had hired had had ample opportunity to size up warriors—few seem to have considered Cody to be much of one.

Once the necessary promotional work had been done and William F. Cody established as the star of stars, he rarely bragged about his Indian killing, and if he did talk about it, it was usually to repeat once again the particulars of the "duel" with Yellow Hair. This set piece was reenacted in many forms, including a movie. The duel with Yellow Hair was, with the Pony Express, the most enduring of all Cody's tropes—it was what would now be called a signature scene.

But showbiz apart, there is every evidence that Bill Cody liked Indians. At the very end, once he essentially belonged to Harry Tammen, he may have liked them better than he liked white people.

5

I HAVE already written that rich people, even royals, just seemed to like Bill Cody. The same might be said of bad people—even the notoriously violent Joseph "Alf" Slade, Cody's boss when he rode for the Pony Express, just seemed to like the kid. Here's Cody's account of their first meeting, when Cody showed up looking for a job:

Among the first persons I saw after dismounting from my horse was Slade. I walked up to him and presented Mr. Russell's letter, which he hastily opened and read. With a sweeping glance of his eye he took my measure from head to foot and then said:

"My boy, you are far too young for a pony express rider. It takes men for that business."

"I rode two months last year on Bill Trotter's division, sir, and filled the bill then; and I think I am better able to ride now."

"What! Are you the boy that was riding there and was called the youngest rider on the road?"

"I am the same boy," I replied, confident now that everything was all right for me.

"I have heard of you before. You are a year or two older now, and I think you can stand it. I'll give you a trial anyhow, and if you weaken you can come back to Horseshoe Station and tend to stock."

That ended our first interview. The next day he assigned me duty on the road from Red Buttes on the North Platte to the Three Crossings on the Sweetwater, a distance of 76 miles, and I began riding at once. It was a long piece of road, but I was equal to the undertaking; and soon after had an opportunity to exhibit my power of endurance as a pony express rider.

One day I galloped into Three Crossings, my home station. I found that the rider who had expected to take the trip on my arrival, had got into a drunken row the night before and been killed; and that there was no one to fill his place. I did not hesitate for a moment to undertake an extra ride of 85 miles to Rocky Ridge, and I arrived at the latter place on time. I then turned and rode back to Red Buttes, my starting place, accomplishing on the round trip a distance of 322 miles.

Slade heard of this feat of mine and one day as he was passing on a coach sang out to me: "My boy, you're a brick and no mistake."

Slade, though rough at times and always a dangerous character—having killed many a man—was always kind to me. During the two years I worked for him as pony express rider and stage driver, he never spoke an angry word to me.

This passage, like the killing of the first Indian, is central to the rapidly swelling legend of Buffalo Bill.

Alf Slade, who never said an unkind word to Cody, seems to have poured hot lead into everybody else. To say that his temper was capricious was akin to saying that Sitting Bull was peevish. Alf Slade is thought to have killed about twenty-six men. If particularly incensed, as he was in at least one case, he might take the trouble to remove his victim's ears, one of which he used as a watch fob. Slade was finally hung by vigilantes in Silver City, Montana—yet he happily sang out a commendation to young Cody.

* * *

Holding that exceptional piece of luck on Cody's part in mind, I should take a moment to consider the brief day of the Pony Express itself. Cody's biographer Don Russell correctly remarks that some sort of mounted delivery system was an old, not a new, thing. If we are to believe Marco Polo, Kublai Khan had some sort of pony express.

Nor was the Pony Express, founded by the firm of Russell, Majors, and Waddell, unique in America in Cody's youth. John Butterfield, whose firm is still in business, pioneered a kind of Big Bend route that nearly touched the Mexican border before curling through the Arizona desert to San Diego. With good luck a letter might be delivered to the West Coast within three or four weeks. However, there were many splendid opportunities for bad luck to happen, in which case the mail never arrived.

Russell, Majors, and Waddell initiated their Pony Express runs in April of 1860—the run started in St. Joseph, Missouri, and edged across country to Sacramento, California. To say that it was hazardous would be to understate. When in full operation the route consisted of 190 stations, five hundred horses, and about eighty riders.

Did Russell, Majors, and Waddell seriously expect to make a profit from this curious venture? Probably not. They were successful freight haulers, transporting freight to various forts or anywhere else, depending on the whim of the client. No doubt they were looking to expand—in particular, to lock up some juicy government contracts. The Pony Express might be effective advertising—at least it might if things went well for a few months. The number of forts in the West was ever increasing—or at least they were until 1868, when Red Cloud and his allies forced the evacuation of three Wyoming forts, all of which had been unwisely situated in the Sioux holy lands.

Russell, Majors, and Waddell probably hoped that the Pony Express—a romantic endeavor if there ever was one—would be excellent advertising, but this seemed to have been a misjudgment on their part. The Pony Express went largely unnoticed at the time. Their young and essentially minor employee Bill Cody in later years reaped many times more publicity from his tour with the Pony Express than did the enterprise itself. He used it as an emblematic element in his shows for over three decades, keeping alive the memory of this short-lived venture for millions who had never heard of it while it was actually in operation.

To this day we lack a fully adequate history of this famous venture—and again, Cody indirectly profited from this lack; many of the details of his Pony Express career can neither be refuted nor confirmed, because of poor documentation.

There are plenty of skeptics who don't believe that Bill Cody rode with the Pony Express at all. One argument against him is the condition that Alf Slade mentioned: Cody's youth. He was only fourteen when the Pony Express runs were initiated, and not quite sixteen when they ended.

Had Cody showed up cold and asked for a job with a company where no one knew him, the age factor might indeed have been decisive. But such was not the case: Cody had already been riding for Russell, Majors, and Waddell for three years; he was known to be an able hand and had already undertaken several cattle-driving expeditions for the firm which were only marginally less dangerous than the Pony Express. In 1860 he was a proven, reliable plainsman whose horsemanship no one doubted.

Still, absolute proof that Cody rode with the Pony Express is elusive. Don Russell manages to find a snatch of testimony that convinces him, though it doesn't convince me. It's a comment from the wealthy Chicago contractor Edward Ayer, the man who formed the wonderful Native American collection now at the Newberry Library in Chicago:

> About six or seven years ago I attended a reception and dinner party given by all the diplomats of Paris to Buffalo Bill. I said it wasn't necessary to introduce me to Bill Cody; that I had crossed the plains in 1860, and he was riding by our train about a month, and would give us the news in a loud voice as he rushed by, so that we became much attached to him. At the reception Bill wouldn't let me get out of his sight, thereby disarranging the seating plan at the banquet.

That snatch is from Edward Ayer's privately printed journal. It seems a very curious passage, to me. Where was the train going, that a Pony Express rider could rush along beside it for about a month? Pony Express runs were not straight runs beside a train track. Why would Cody, isolated as he was in remote places, have "news" that a Chicago businessman wouldn't have? And how would Cody become so familiar with Ayer, whom he had only glimpsed through a train window, that he could recognize him at a banquet in Paris two and a half decades later?

I don't think Ayer's comment proves anything at all about Buffalo Bill and the Pony Express, but I *am* inclined to think he did ride with it, since that would merely have been a more or less natural extension of a job he already had.

The first rider out of St. Joseph may have been Bob Haslam, whom Cody would later employ in his Wild West shows—in fact he went on to employ a surprising number of prairie characters he had known in his years on the plains.

On literary grounds, too, I'm inclined to think that Cody's Pony Express work was real, if possibly exaggerated. The passages about Pony Express work are much less theatrically written than the passages about Indian fights or Indian killing. There's less conflation, more of a feel that Cody might have written this part himself.

The 322-mile ride he claimed—that's about the distance from Los Angeles to Phoenix—is thought to be the third-longest made during the brief, eighteen-month life of the Pony Express. The longest ride, 384 miles, was made by Bob Haslam, who lived to re-create it in many arenas. The second-longest, 330 miles, was made by one Howard Egan. Cody, at 322 miles, comes in third. He seems to have once thought he made a 384-mile ride, and one of his sisters clings to that figure, but it resulted from a clear miscalculation of his routes. Arithmetic was never one of the great scout's strong suits.

The Pony Express per se was in business from April of 1860 until November of 1861. The owners knew they were racing the telegraph, and the telegraph soon beat them: The two coasts were linked in November of 1860—the singing wires, as the Indians called them, had come to stay.

Buffalo Bill's 322-mile ride took twenty-two hours and was accomplished with the help of twenty-one horses, which suggests that he got about an hour's hard work out of each horse.

Most writing about the Pony Express emphasizes how hard the work was on the riders, but little has been written about the horses that made the enterprise possible. Initially the stations had been twenty-five miles apart, but it was soon lowered to about half that distance—too few horses were able to go hard for twenty-five miles. (Some Indians were said to be able to get fifty to seventy-five miles out of a horse, after which, probably, they ate the exhausted animal—this too is probably an exaggeration.)

Cody often mentions his mounts, a few of whose names have come down to us. When some Indians jumped him near Horse Creek on one ride he mentions that he was mounted on "a roan California horse, the fleetest steed I had." Agnes Wright Spring has produced a pamphlet about Cody's horses, the most famous of which was his buffalo-shooting horse Brigham. Two other horses from his scouting days were Buckskin Joe and Charlie. Buckskin Joe eventually went blind, presumably from having to carry Cody nearly two hundred miles on one ride. Isham was the most famous of the show horses. Harry Tammen callously sold Isham at the sheriff's sale, along with the rest of Cody's livestock, but some friends bought the old horse back and presented him to the old rider.

I mention the horses because, clearly, Cody's horsemanship, and his judgment about the speed and staying power of his mounts, was essential to his survival.

The otherwise vicious and homicidal Alf Slade took such a shine to young Cody that he decided to keep him at his own station and only use him as a kind of supernumerary rider—a curious word to come out of the mouth of such a rough old sort, but that's the word Cody reports.

Life at Horseshoe Station being comparatively easy, Cody one day decides to venture out on a bear hunt—or as he puts it:

> One day, when I had nothing else to do, I saddled up an extra Pony Express horse, and arming myself with a good rifle and a pair of revolvers, struck out for the foothills of Laramie Peak for a bear hunt. Riding carelessly along, and

breathing the cool and bracing autumn air which came down from the mountains, I felt as only a man can feel who is roaming over the prairies of the far West, well armed and mounted on a fleet and gallant steed. The perfect freedom he enjoys is in itself a refreshing stimulant to the mind as well as the body. Such indeed were my feelings on this beautiful day, as I rode up the valley of the Horseshoe.

The day continues beautiful and eventually turns into night without Cody having stirred up any bears. What he locates, instead, is a meadow with fifteen or twenty horses grazing in it. Prudence might have suggested to the young man that he turn and skedaddle, but he chooses to investigate and soon finds himself in a den of horse thieves, encamped in a kind of cave. Some of the men he recognizes as having been discharged from a freighting company he is familiar with. Cody soon realizes he is in a tight spot; he has left his horse some distance away and offers to leave his rifle with the men while he recovers the animal. The ruffians are happy to take the rifle but have no intention of leaving Cody any chance to escape. Two men go with him to fetch the horse, one in front of him and one behind. The men had not bothered to search him and do not know about the two pistols. As they are leading his horse up to the meadow Cody manages to drop a sage hen he had killed earlier in the day. When the man behind him stops to pick it up Cody whacks him hard with the pistol and turns just in time to shoot the man ahead of him, killing him dead. Then he flees into some rocky foothill country—his horse has to be abandoned but he makes good his escape.

Now, Cody had many narrow escapes in his career on the prairies. Even as early as nine he was forced to flee a group of thugs calling themselves the Border Ruffians, a primitive, violently proslavery vigilante group who wanted to do violence to young Billy because he was the son of a man they considered to be an abolitionist.

Always, though, young Cody just escapes—almost as the hero might do at the end of a movie serial. The Border Ruffians he manages to outrun until he reaches the home of friends, leaving his pursuers to retreat empty-handed.

All of Cody's pursuers, whether white or Indian, from the mid-fifties on to the late seventies, are forced to retreat empty-handed. Cody always has a better horse, or knows the country better; he keeps a cool head and manages to escape.

He admitted to being scared when he shot the first Indian, and he was no doubt not happy to have stumbled into the cave of the horse thieves—if he did—but the evidence suggests that Cody really did keep an uncommonly cool head, and this despite the fact that he was frequently drunk. Cody's drinking I'll discuss a little later, but his ability to either outrun or else hide from people who were pursuing him with deadly intent manifests itself often in his book. In most cases the reader is not inclined to doubt him. Plenty of people traveling those prairies did get chased in those times; working as Cody did, where and when he did, meant that rapid flight was more or less part of his job skills.

The den-of-thieves incident reads very dime-novel-like, but its main significance, if it happened, is that it marked the only time in his life when Cody claims to have killed a white man.

As if suspecting that some readers might want to verify such a claim, he goes on to mention that Alf Slade and a well-armed group followed him back to the site—the horses and the horse thieves were gone but there was a fresh grave in the meadow, presumably the final resting place of the man Cody shot.

In the autobiography, only a page or two earlier, there is an amusing illustration of Alf Slade summarily gunning down a stage-coach driver who had managed to offend him. Alf Slade always felt free to dispense his own justice, as did the vigilantes in Montana when they hung him.

Apart from the fact that his job with the Pony Express required Cody to ride farther and faster than he would normally have done, it didn't really change the customary pattern of his life very much. He would likely have been somewhere on the central plains of the West, riding horses, scouting, hunting, delivering messages for some military man—maybe General Carr or General Sheridan—or some hauling company.

One of his more ballsy efforts was his successful attempt to get the Sioux chief Spotted Tail (uncle of Crazy Horse) to come south and put on a little show—sham fighting, real killing of buffalo from horseback with bow and arrow, some dancing—as entertainment for the grand duke Alexis on his much-publicized visit. Though Spotted Tail himself was friendly to whites, plenty of his young warriors were much less so and would have been glad to take Cody's scalp had they run into him on his way north. Yet Cody got away with his rather daring infiltration and the Sioux came and did their bit to entertain a nobleman from a country they had never heard of.

Cody was active, he was able, he was trusted by both the army and the freight companies, and he accepted several courier jobs in country dangerous enough that most men might have declined the assignment. All through his youth and young manhood he worked mostly alone, breathing the cool free air of the prairies.

It was when first youth had passed, and the plains life became less and less free, that Cody, like many another plainsman, trapper, or meat hunter of his generation, came to realize that he would soon have to find another way to make a living. What Bill Cody recognized, more acutely than most of his contemporaries, was that all most Americans would know of the great adventure of the American West was whatever he could bring to them in his Wild West shows; he also figured out that a nearly ideal place to start would be the Pony Express—after all, what would be more appealing than the sight of the racing riders of the Pony Express? As a business, it hadn't worked out, but as a spectacle it thrilled audiences everywhere.

William F. Cody in young manhood.

Cody at the height of his fame.

Cody reenacting the taking of the first scalp for Custer, his Indian War Pictures, 1913.

Cody on a mock buffalo hunt.

4

BUFFALO BILL'S WILD WEST

AND

Congress of Rough Riders of the World.

ADMIT ONE.

Personal Courtesy.

Compliments of

Chicago, 1893.

B. B. W. W.

Personal Courtesy.

ADMIT ONE.

GRAND STAND.

JOHN M. BURKE,
Gen'l Manager.

*A ticket to Buffalo
Bill's Wild West.*

*Annie Oakley
promotional
photograph.*

Annie Oakley in a stage pose about 1880.

7

Annie Oakley giving a shooting lesson.

8

Louisa Cody about the time of her marriage.

9

The Codys in their sixties.

10

Ned Buntline, Buffalo Bill, the peerless Morlacchi, and Texas Jack Omohundro as they appeared on stage.

James Butler (Wild Bill) Hickok.

13

Major John Burke, Cody's loyal press agent.

Red Cloud and Major Burke.

14

Nate Salsbury, the formidable manager of the Wild West.

15

Top row: Julius Meyer, Red Cloud.
Bottom row: Sitting Bull, Swift Bear,
Spotted Tail.

Black Elk, the Ogalala sage.

6

Two things young Bill Cody had very little use for were practical soldiering and politics. His father, Isaac, had been quite political, with a good attendance record in the fledgling territorial legislature, but it is hard to find anything in Cody's autobiography or his various interviews that could be considered a political statement. He soldiered, usually rather listlessly and in a ragtag way, with the Seventh Kansas and, somewhat later, with the Fifth Cavalry and one or two other units. Real military fervor, of the sort Sherman had, or Custer, was simply absent from Cody's makeup. In 1889 he was made a brigadier general—this was when he was invited by General Miles to take a hand in the Ghost Dance troubles, an invitation that, perhaps foolishly, was reversed before Cody ever reached Sitting Bull's camp; but he preferred the title of Colonel, a rank he never officially held. It seems he simply awarded it to himself when he realized that his pay equaled a colonel's pay: so why couldn't he have the rank?

The terrible Civil War, a war that was ripping the nation apart, didn't seem to much excite Cody, one way or another. His prejudices and his loyalties were essentially local. He had promised his mother that he wouldn't enlist while she was alive, and he kept his promise, though he did some irregular scouting during the early years of the war. Mary Laycock Cody died in 1863.

Among Cody's strong and specific prejudices was a dislike of Missourians, whom he blamed for the death of his father. Becoming a Jayhawker—Kansans of a rough nature who stole horses from

Confederates and sometimes sold them to the Unionists and other times just sold them. Rougher even than the Jayhawkers were the Red Legged Scouts, so called because their leggings were made from a red sheepskin popular with shoemakers in those days. The Red Legged Scouts were mainly just thieves and murderers, as young Bill Cody soon realized. He blamed his involvement on drunkenness, which he was much given to in those days. James Butler (later Wild Bill) Hickok became friendly with Cody around this time and even stayed as a guest in the hotel the Cody family was attempting to run in the Salt Creek Valley. Cody and Hickok were to remain buddies throughout the Civil War and afterward. Hickok eventually became a Union spy but at first he was, like Cody, not much excited by the war.

It may be that Cody and Hickok's rather lackadaisical attitude toward the war was due to their lack of proximity to the real action. Near the end of the war, in 1864, Cody occasionally did get drawn into some fairly sharp action near Independence, Missouri. Later in life, when in a tale-telling mood, he claimed to have been in a scouting party that captured Major General John Sappington Marmaduke near the Marais des Cygnes River, the so-called Swamp of the Swans, where the great tundra swans come, an area beloved by birdwatchers today. According to Cody he and General Marmaduke shared lunch and a bottle of whiskey.

Cody served a little more than a year and a half with the Seventh Kansas. On mustering out he was still a private. There is no evidence that he ever acquired much interest in military protocol, and he seems to have had even less interest in military training. What he had to offer the army—any army—was his knowledge of the country; he knew how to get from here to there, and could usually do so even if hostilities were in progress.

Though he liked to brag a little about his lunch with General Marmaduke, Cody was not vainglorious about his soldiering—and the same could be said for his Indian fighting. Frequently he would remark of a particular skirmish or chase that, really, it didn't amount to much—in these instances he was truthful. Many short engagements didn't amount to much.

Cody, who could be quite specific about details if he chose to

be, could never quite remember actually enlisting in the Seventh
Kansas. In Leavenworth, after his mother's death, he

> entered upon a dissolute and reckless life—to my shame,
> be it said—and associated with gamblers, drunkards, and
> bad characters generally. I continued my dissipation about
> two months and was become a very hard case—I met
> quite a number of my old comrades and neighbors, who
> tried to enduce me to enlist and go south with them. I had
> no intention of doing anything of the kind; but one day,
> after having been under the influence of bad whiskey, I
> awoke to find myself a soldier in the Seventh Kansas.

He enlisted in February of 1864, which was rather late in the
war. But for the bad whiskey he might never have enlisted at all.

7

BECAUSE Bill Cody, by the standards of our time, started work so young, and because the highlighted episodes—what I have called the tropes—so much dominate the story of his fame, it's easy to forget that the narrative of his life is one story and the narrative of his fame another.

When Cody obliviously enlisted in the Seventh Kansas he was only eighteen. He had quit the Pony Express in 1861 and was for a time at loose ends, rather in the manner of teenagers everywhere. Cody just happened to be a good deal more experienced than most teenagers would have been. When he was thirteen his mother actually got him to go to school for two months, the longest period of instruction he ever suffered.

This brief educational interlude ended when the Colorado gold rush caused gold fever to flare up across the nation. It was Pikes Peak or bust for many an American youth. Cody rushed off west with some friends, none of whom knew the slightest thing about mining. Very soon they were bust. Fortunately Cody ran into a wagon master he had worked for previously; once again he found himself a teamster, working his way home.

It was about this time that Mrs. Cody turned the Cody home into a hotel, a short-lived effort. The few guests she could lure in were mostly just her son's friends, Wild Bill Hickok among them.

Mining having failed, young Cody next turned to trapping, partnering with Dave Harrington, who had briefly been one of his lively sister Julia's suitors. This was in 1859, just before his Pony Express job. The beaver boom had ended some decades previously, mainly because the beaver themselves were more or less ended—though there were still a few rich pockets of these valuable rodents. Probably there was a good deal of nostalgia in the Cody-Harrington expedition—yearning of a sort that sometimes seizes thirteen-year-olds. It gave the boys a chance to feel that they were actually of the mountain man generation, which they may have fantasized about much as young cowboys will still fantasize about having been trail drivers. Cody idolized Kit Carson and was probably seeking at least a taste of Carson's experience.

At any rate Cody and Harrington were soon trapping the Republican River, in Colorado. Though they had an ox team and abundant supplies, luck did not attend their efforts. One ox slipped on some ice, dislocated a hip, and had to be shot. Then a bear attacked the other ox. Cody managed to shoot the bear, but then he too slipped on the ice and broke his leg. Harrington set the leg but winter was upon them. They made a fairly snug dugout in the side of a hill, after which it was decided that Harrington should leave Cody and go for help. They reckoned that he could probably make the necessary round trip in about three weeks, but bad weather intervened and it was twenty-nine days before Cody saw Dave Harrington again.

Cody had abundant supplies—at least he did for a while—and weathered the interval well enough but for one close call, a visit by a party of Sioux who were on the prowl. Probably they would have made short work of this boy had it not been for the fortunate intervention of a Sioux elder Cody had happened to meet at Fort Laramie during one of his hauls.

The Sioux elder was old Rain in the Face, who—at least as the trope has it—intervened and persuaded the hostile warriors to spare the young man's life. The warriors submitted grudgingly. They took Cody's guns and the lion's share of his provisions, but they didn't kill him.

Dime-novelish as this story sounds, it was more than likely true. The young trappers were in a country thick with Sioux, and a leader, or at least an elder, named Rain in the Face did exist. His son, young Rain in the Face, fought in the Battle of the Little Bighorn and, for a time, claimed to have fired the shot that killed Custer. This claim is no longer given much credit. Sitting Bull pointed out that everyone was shooting at Custer (though his body bore only two bullet wounds).

In his book Cody expresses considerable annoyance at the Indians for making free with his possessions, though they could readily have made just as free with his life. Being saved by old Rain in the Face made a good tableau in the Wild West shows, but the incident, assuming it happened, was actually one of Cody's narrowest escapes—if the old Sioux hadn't remembered him, or if he had just chosen to stay in his lodge that day, it is doubtful that there would have been many legends of Buffalo Bill.

8

THERE was one significant aspect of his life that Buffalo Bill Cody could never convert into a trope or reduce to a playlet in his Wild West shows, and that was his long, mostly turbulent marriage to Louisa Frederici, a comely St. Louis girl of French descent. In her youth Lulu was both very attractive and very spirited.

The two were introduced by Lulu's cousins in a somewhat awkward way. Cody and the cousin walked in, found Lulu dozing over a book, and promptly jerked the chair out from under her—Cody never quite determined the right way to approach women. Louisa, meaning to slap her cousin, slapped Cody instead. Since Louisa had a date that evening with a gentleman she didn't really want to see, she persuaded Cody to stick around and help her pretend that she and Cody were engaged.

According to Louisa, this auspicious meeting occurred in May 1865.

Forty years later, when he was trying unsuccessfully to divorce Lulu, Cody had this to say about the mock engagement: "Boylike, I thought it very smart to be engaged. I asked her to marry me, or asked her if she would marry me if I would come back after the war was over. And jokingly she said yes."

If the engagement really began in May of 1865, then of course the war *was* over, though Cody, who had never been much interested in the war, may not have taken in this fact. Cody was on the move, as usual, and claimed to be a little surprised when he got home to Leav-

61

enworth and found several letters from Lulu, asking him to keep his word. Perhaps surprisingly, he *did* keep his word. In the divorce proceedings in 1905 he tried to pretend he was tricked into a marriage he never wanted, but a passage in the autobiography was there to trip him up: "I returned to St. Louis, having made up my mind to capture the heart of Miss Frederici, whom I adored above any young lady I had ever seen."

Louisa's heart *was* captured, and the two were very soon married, but it was not long before Louisa had an inkling that the ruse of their engagement may have chased off the wrong suitor. Just as the boat was pulling out, to take the honeymooners upriver to Leavenworth, a gang of ruffians rushed at them. Someone had recognized Cody from his jayhawking days and proposed to hang him then and there, an impulse Louisa soon came to sympathize with. Accustomed from birth to the amenities of the old French Quarter in St. Louis, she was unprepared for the amenityless village that Leavenworth then was. She was also unprepared for Bill's rough acquaintances, some sixty of whom were at the dock with a brass band when their boat pulled in, eager to perform a kind of prairie charivari, a practice that probably came as a big shock to the gently bred Louisa.

This is not to say that Louisa Cody lacked the fighting spirit; where Bill Cody was concerned she could more than take up for herself—when she could catch him, that is. But Bill, true to his nature, was usually on the move. At one point he guided General Sherman, then commander of the Division of the Mississippi, from Fort Riley to Fort Kearny—much later Sherman thanked him by giving him a blurb for his Wild West show. It's a safe guess that Cody's thoughts turned none too often to the young bride he had left at home in Leavenworth.

Louisa had nothing of the pioneer in her. She missed city pleasures and city ways. And she missed her husband. If Bill Cody had at least stayed home to fight with her she might have stuck it out in Leavenworth, but with him gone most of the time and their first child coming, she, sensibly, took herself back to St. Louis. Bill Cody accepted this move as nonchalantly as he had accepted the end of the Civil War. He liked St. Louis himself—the prairie just happened to be the place where he made his living.

Children came, riches came, mistresses came—some of them very expensive mistresses, such as the actress Katherine Clemmons, whose meager talent Cody spent some $80,000 promoting—but Louisa was still his wife, housed at first in tents and barracks, then later in grand houses in North Platte, Nebraska, or Rochester, New York, but not very happy in any of the above. The boy they took in, Dan Muller, loved Louisa and wrote poignantly of the sadness he felt when she informed him that she could no longer live with Uncle Bill. Yet the union, despite Bill's strange attempt to end it in its fortieth year (when Louisa revealed her jealousy of Queen Victoria), remained somehow a marriage.

In writing about two other classically difficult marriages—those of the Carlyles and the Tolstoys—the critic V. S. Pritchett spoke of these tightly bound yet eternally warring couples as "the professionals of marriage." But the Carlyles and the Tolstoys faced their difficulties in lockstep, under the same roof, whereas Louisa's principal difficulty was in keeping Bill home for any length of time. When old Count Tolstoy finally wandered off from Yasnaya Polyana, he left a venerable, long-established country seat. Bill Cody had no such seat, although he built several great piles that might have served as one had he been a settled person. But he had grown up as a virtual nomad on the wild free prairies and it was a liking for the nomad's life, rather than a dislike of his wife, that kept him on the move. For most of his life he made his living through nomadic pursuits, and this didn't really change when he became an impresario. The shows still had to move. And Cody had to move. It is doubtful that he could have stayed put for a whole year even if there was a big stipend to be earned.

Louisa soon learned to be practical in her abandonment. As soon as Cody had money he began to buy property; at least he would if he could close a deal before he squandered the money. When she saw this pattern emerging Louisa soon developed a rather good head for business, which, in this case, meant seeing that all of the property was put in her name, a fact Cody didn't notice until he ran into financial difficulties in the eighties and nineties.

Bill and Louisa's fights were on a par with the Tolstoys'—many were as ridiculous as any farce ever staged, but like most marital fights, they were only funny if one happened to be a spectator, not a player. Bill Cody was never really indifferent to Lulu; their children came and there were times when he recovered his early affection for her, but it didn't keep him from being gone a lot, leaving a restless woman stuck on the lonely plains.

In their fifty-one years of marriage it is doubtful that Cody was home even for six months at a stretch. He missed births—he even missed deaths. They were together so irregularly that they never fully got used to one another—every time Bill came home there would have to be an awkward period of readjustment to their domestic state. At the very end, after all the fights, all the mistresses, all the long estrangements, were the war-worn Codys glad that they had one another still?

The question is hard to answer because no biographer with much psychological acuteness has troubled to look hard at the Cody marriage. The complexities of Bill's career really overshadowed it. In 1920, three years after Cody's death, Lulu wrote a little memoir with the help of Courtney Ryley Cooper, Annie Oakley's first biographer. It's a readable effort, though with some massive gaps and a good deal of vagueness and imprecision. Lulu Cody had lived in North Platte, Nebraska, for some thirty-five years and yet seemed to believe that the town and also Bill's ranch were close to the Wyoming line. They weren't.

The source most likely to tell the reader what Lulu Cody's life was like is a book by the diminutive (four foot eight) but vigorous Nebraska historian Nellie Snyder Yost. Her book is called *Buffalo Bill: His Family, Friends, Fame, Failures, and Fortunes*—it's not as good on Cody himself as the books by Don Russell and Joy Kasson, but it's much better than either of those on the Codys' home life, to the extent that they had one.

Nellie Snyder Yost had the advantage of living on the spot— North Platte, Nebraska—where much of the Codys' domestic life took place. She knew several Codys, and of course heard many tales. To this day Buffalo Bill is a huge presence in North Platte—in a way he's the only presence, even now. Nellie Yost has done her best to separate truth from rumor, something that becomes harder and harder to do as the years pass. I doubt that she's one hundred percent successful—no biographer is—but she comes a good deal closer than either Bill or Lulu has done. Somehow she gets the feel of what the prairie scout and his often left at home wife really felt about one another.

Lulu Cody's book, *Memories of Buffalo Bill by His Wife,* is interesting in part because of what it leaves out. Annie Oakley is never mentioned and neither is Katherine Clemmons or any of the six old girlfriends who showed up at Cody's funeral. On the page, at least, Lulu finally had Bill Cody to herself.

9

FROM 1857, when he began to work for Russell, Majors, and Waddell, William F. Cody could fairly be described as an able all-round plainsman. He could drive teams, he could cowboy, he was a sought-after courier, he was a more than competent hunter as well as an organizer of hunts. He could fight Indians if required, although he clearly preferred to live and let live where the Indians were concerned. But when the Civil War ended he was still a youth, essentially unestablished, just one more mustered-out private.

Then along came the dime novelist Ned Buntline, who sensed a different potential for Bill Cody. It was Buntline who first nudged Cody toward what would become a brilliant career as a showman, a career that would occupy him during the second half of his life.

His fame as Buffalo Bill, however, was forged on the plains, during the half decade between 1866 and 1871, when Cody, without exactly pushing himself, managed to receive major publicity for what looks now to have been a very minor role in the almost constant Indian wars that were fought on the great plains during these critical years.

A word of background may be helpful.

When the Civil War finally ended America was a war-weary nation. A few years of peace would not have been amiss, and yet, only in the industrial Northeast was there much peace. The South was soon engulfed in the struggles of Reconstruction, and in the West there were a goodly number of very warlike tribes who were by this time awake to the fact that their way of life was under serious threat.

A few privileged Indian leaders—Red Cloud, Spotted Tail, Sitting Bull, and others—thanks to the government's shrewd policy of bringing such leaders east, to show them the majesty of Washington and New York, with perhaps a visit to the president thrown in, knew that what lay ahead for their people was more in the nature of a promise than a threat: but a deadly promise it was, as Red Cloud recognized. Late in his life he remarked that the whites had made many promises, more than he could remember, but they had only kept one. They said they would take the Indians' land, and they took it.

Sitting Bull, after coming to Washington and meeting with President Cleveland, recognized immediately that there was really no hope. The Indians would have to do what the white men wanted them to do, and live where they wanted them to live, or the Indians would die.

Even if every Indian killed a white man with every step he took, Sitting Bull said, it would change nothing. The whites were too many, the Indians too few; besides which, the whites had better weapons.

Still, no matter how clear their insight, or how grave their doubts about the future, the Plains Indians were warrior societies, and they were defending homelands and long-held traditions which they loved. So they were going to fight. They were warriors, it was their country, they knew it better than even the best white scouts; for a time there would be wholesale war.

The white soldier with perhaps the clearest strategic vision where the Indians were concerned was General William Tecumseh Sherman, who shortly after the Civil War ended was made commander of the Department of the Mississippi. Sherman's way of fighting impressed itself on the nation in his great, deadly march to the sea. War was hell; the more brutal it could be made, the quicker it would be over.

In the settled South there was no escape, if one happened to be in Sherman's path.

But the West was not the settled South. The Indians were skilled mobile fighting units; they didn't have plantations or small farms that could be torched—though when an American commander did happen to hit a well-supplied village, as Crook did in Montana in 1875, the soldiers did burn everything, including foodstuffs that they themselves would later come to need.

Sherman may have been the first to realize that the advance of the railroads would very shortly doom the Indians. Most of them, with the buffalo they depended on, would be caught between the Union Pacific and the Northern Pacific. If one hunter, Buffalo Bill Cody, could kill three thousand buffalo in a short space of time, what chance did the buffalo have when whole trainloads of professional hunters could come right to the herds by rail? No chance, of course; the buffalo would vanish and the soon-to-be-starving Indians would have to do as they were told.

Sherman's theory was flawless—the only difficulty was political. The tracks of the two railroads were rapidly getting laid, but would-be settlers, thousands of them, were making tracks of their own at an even more rapid rate. Westering became a national compulsion; there was no stopping the tide of immigrants along the Platte, across the Santa Fe Trail, or any way that seemed convenient at the moment.

Ahead of these immigrants lay many dangers, but no danger greater than the aroused fury of the Plains Indians. The U.S. Army, tired and depleted though it may have been in the first postwar decade, was very soon being asked to make a safe way for all the white folks seeking land.

Sherman had no tolerance for Indians who wouldn't behave. His policy was clearly exterminationist; it may be that he best expressed it in a letter he sent to General Phil Sheridan as the great battle for the plains was about to be joined:

> As brave men and as the soldiers of a government which has exhausted the peace efforts, we, in the performance of a most unpleasant duty, accept the war begun by our enemies, and hereby resolve to make its end final. If it results in the utter annihilation of these Indians it is but the result of what they have been warned against again and again, and for which they seem fully prepared. I will do nothing to restrain our troops from doing what they deem

proper on the spot, and will allow no mere vague general charges of cruelty and inhumanity to tie their hands, but will use all the powers confided in me to the end that these Indians, the enemies of our race and our civilization, shall not again be able to begin and carry on their barbarous warfare on any kind of pretense that they may choose to allege . . . You may now go ahead in your own way and I will back you with my whole authority, and stand between you and any efforts that may be attempted in your rear to restrain your purpose or check your troops.

Sherman may have been referring to the Peace Party, those Congressmen or politicians who felt there should be an effort to find a middle ground with the Indian tribes. For this movement, which was not wholly ineffective, Sherman had nothing but contempt. He is one of three individuals to whom the bluntest of all policy statements—that the only good Indian is a dead Indian—has been attributed. The first to say it was probably the Montana congressman James Cavanaugh; then Sheridan picked it up, and finally Sherman, who (according to Mencken) said it to an Indian who was panhandling at a railway station as Sherman was disembarking. "Me good Indian," the old man said, to which Sherman replied, "So far as I know the only good Indian is a dead Indian." It is doubtful that the old panhandler received a cent.

The harshness of Sherman's policy where Indians were concerned accounts for the fact that George Armstrong Custer, despite a court-martial or two and many callous infringements of military rules, kept being called back to command in the West. The fact that he abandoned Major Joel Elliott and eighteen men at the time of the Washita battle was not forgotten by either the officers or the rank and file, but Custer shrugged it off. He was by no means as able a commander as Sherman but his willingness to fight was evident to all. In a sense he lived to fight. He was harsh to and hated by his men, as well as by most of his fellow officers, but he was, nonetheless, the kind of man Sherman was looking for: one to whom fighting came first.

When President Lincoln, sorely beset at the outset of the Civil

War by dithering generals, began to receive reports of victory after victory secured by the nearly unknown Ulysses S. Grant, he said, in admiration: "He fights."

Exactly the same could be said for Custer, although Grant was reliable and Custer wildly erratic: he might simply ride off from his command to go have a romantic tryst with his wife—he did this in Kansas—but fighting was what he liked to do best, and he always returned to it once his critical superiors had been appeased. Sheridan moved mountains to get Custer out of his various scrapes; he wanted him back in the West. Yet Custer's achievements in the West, once you boil them down, amount to very little.

His one victory was the Battle of the Washita, and how wise a victory was that? He succeeded in killing Black Kettle, the most famous peace Indian of his time. A few warriors were killed but most of the dead were women and children. His reconnaissance, as usual, was feeble; it was only after he wrapped up Black Kettle's village that Custer realized that the part of the plains where he was seemed to be swarming with Indians. He at once hustled back to a less exposed position, having achieved his one and only victory in the Plains Indian wars—and achieved it against the one Indian who didn't want to fight.

Black Kettle's tough wife was also killed in this battle, though their two bodies were not immediately identified. During the terrible massacre at Sand Creek, Black Kettle's wife had received no less than nine wounds, but Black Kettle somehow managed to carry her the forty miles to Fort Lyon, where the doctors saved her.

It would be almost eight years before George Armstrong Custer led his gallant Seventh Cavalry against another Indian village. This was on a Montana plain in June of 1876, and when it was over, "Long Hair comes no more," the Indian women sang.

10

THAT General Sherman was philosophically willing to totally exterminate the Plains Indians was clear enough from the letter quoted, and from numerous other statements. He would have been glad to mow them down and plow them under, but when he actually began to put armies in the field in 1866–1867, it soon became obvious that he didn't have the muscle to accomplish any such genocidal program.

The Confederate soldiers against whom Sherman had made his reputation as a fighting general mainly stood and fought, dying if necessary. But the Sioux, the Cheyenne, the Pawnee, the Comanche, the Kiowa, the Arapaho, the Apache, and so forth much preferred to fight and run. When sent to retaliate for some raid or other, the U.S. Army could rarely catch the Indians they were after. They were not particularly well provisioned, and in any case, were temperamentally unsuited to long pursuits. The chases were frustrating, so much so that the soldiers usually fell back on punishing any Indians they happened to run into. Since their high command was on record as believing that the only good Indian was a dead Indian, why discriminate?

In time, though, there would appear officers of the highest caliber, such as General George Crook, who *did* discriminate. General Crook, on his tours of duty in Arizona, spent a lot of time sorting out the Apache situation. There were nine branches of the Apache peoples; Crook's distinction was that he took care not to punish the wrong tribes. He was fair, the Apaches realized it, and Crook came to be treated with respect. And the northern Indians, too, mostly respected Crook, particularly after they spent a whole day whipping up on him at the Battle of the Rosebud in 1876.

As for the fire-breathing William Tecumseh Sherman, irony soon overtook his effort to secure the northern plains. It soon became apparent that he didn't have the manpower, which forced him into tedious negotiations and slow diplomacy, tasks for which he was not well suited. Sherman probably sat through more peace pow-wows than any other general. His principal opponent in these debates, the Ogalala Red Cloud, was noted for his long-winded oratory. He might talk half the day—on the other hand, he might not bother to show up at all. If some buffalo crossed his path while he was on the way to a powwow he might decide to hunt first and negotiate later.

When he did arrive Red Cloud made it clear that if the whites wanted peace they needed to stop building forts in the Sioux lands. Three such forts—Fort Reno, Fort Phil Kearny, and Fort C. F. Smith—had foolishly been built right in the Sioux holy lands. There had been a gold strike in Montana—the three forts were supposed to protect immigrants along the Bozeman Trail. But the forts' defenses were so weak that the army was forced to abandon them in 1868—although many warriors owing no allegiance to Red Cloud were involved in harassing the forts, the victory was attributed to Red Cloud and the episode became known as Red Cloud's War.

The victory, of course, was pyrrhic—the slackening on the part of the U.S. military was only temporary. Within a decade of the closing of those forts, Custer was dead, Spotted Tail was dead, Crazy Horse was dead, Sitting Bull was in Canada, Buffalo Bill had had his famous "duel" with Yellow Hair, and except for a few stubborn Apaches in the rocks of Arizona and New Mexico, the contest for the Western lands was over. A decade after Custer lost his last command, Geronimo and his eighteen warriors came in. The great contest was over, though paranoia about Indian intentions and capabilities was not quick to subside. Out of just such paranoia came the more or less meaningless flare-up in 1890, at Wounded Knee. Again for reasons of paranoia—administrative this time—the by then world-famous Buffalo Bill Cody was prevented from meeting his old star, Sitting Bull, soon to be killed by native policemen.

Much later Cody made a movie about Wounded Knee, but few came to see it.

11

HELEN CODY WETMORE, Cody's younger sister, titled her
rose-colored biography of her brother *The Last of the Great
Scouts*. Was Cody a great scout, and if so, what does that mean?

Again, a little background might help. One of the most ineffec-
tual military campaigns mounted in the post–Civil War West was
that under the command of General Winfield Scott Hancock, which
lumbered off into the central plains in 1867, spinning off, as it went,
many smaller commands, some of which promptly got lost. Skeptics
might argue that General Hancock himself was lost for much of this
campaign. He was, however, the overall commander. Wherever he
happened to find himself became true north, in a sense.

Why this large, unwieldy force thought it could catch up with
and punish small, highly mobile groups of Native American horsemen is one of those military mysteries that can never be explained.
Sherman, realist in military matters, can hardly have placed much
faith in this expedition. Sheridan, a major participant, was often
vexed by the difficulty of engaging the enemy in numbers that might
have made the whole thing cost effective. General Hancock and
many of his semidetached commands mostly floundered around to
no purpose, trying to sift through the ever-shifting mass of rumor in
hopes of locating a grain or two of usable intelligence that might
eventually lead them to an Indian.

Here, for example, is an indication of the use Sheridan was able
to make of Cody, upon receiving the unwelcome news that the Co-

manches and the Kiowa were on the warpath, information that needed to be conveyed to central command, or at least *some* command, as quickly as possible:

> This intelligence required that certain orders should be carried to Fort Dodge, ninety-five miles south of Hays. This too being a particularly dangerous route—several couriers having been killed on it—it was impossible to get one of the various "Petes," "Jacks," or "Jims" hanging around Hays City to take any communication. Cody learning of the strait I was in, manfully came to the rescue and proposed to make the trip to Dodge, though he had just finished his long and perilous ride from Larned. I gratefully accepted his offer, and after four or five hours rest he mounted a fresh horse and hastened on his journey, halting but once to rest on the way, and then only for an hour, the stop being made at Coon Creek, where he got another mount from a troop of cavalry. At Dodge he took six hours sleep and then continued on to his own post—Fort Larned—with more dispatches. After resting for twelve hours at Larned, he was again in the saddle with tidings for me at Fort Hays, General Hazen sending him this time, with word that the villagers had fled to the south of the Arkansas. Thus, in all, Cody rode about 350 miles in less than sixty hours, and such an exhibition of endurance and courage was more than enough to convince me that his services would be extremely valuable in the campaign, so I retained him at Fort Hays until the battalion of the Fifth Cavalry arrived and then made him chief of scouts of that regiment.

Don Russell, a careful map reader, corrected General Sheridan's arithmetic, concluding that Cody only rode 290 miles on this particular circuit, not 350, but it still works out to an average of 116 miles a day, no mean pace, and a pace maintained through country where he might have encountered hostile Indians at any time.

General Eugene Carr was also impressed with Cody's daring,

and with his ability to cover country. He called Cody the "best white trailer" he had ever worked with. General Carr took over the Fifth Cavalry during this campaign and used Cody often.

Of course Cody, as courier, was merely doing the job he had been doing since the age of eleven. He had by this time had plenty of training, and was thoroughly familiar with the country he was crossing. He seems to have had an excellent inner compass and was apparently never lost, a characteristic he shared with the great Texas cattleman Charles Goodnight, a plainsman also noted for his ability to chew up ground. And yet General Sheridan was surely right to applaud Cody, for he *was* taking very substantial risks. At least five times in the autobiography he finds himself in a race for his life, races that, as I have said, he only narrowly won. Some Kiowa under the important chief Satanta were once after him nip and tuck, one Kiowa coming so close that Cody was forced to shoot the horse out from under him.

One of the "authentic" aspects of Cody's life as a scout was his often repeated decision to aim for the horse rather than the rider— the horse obviously made a considerably bigger target. Indeed, students who don't think Cody actually killed Yellow Hair agree that he did shoot his horse out from under him, making him much more killable.

Cody, as a performer, often loped around one arena or another, shooting glass balls with a smoothbore rifle whose cartridges were filled with birdshot, an easy enough thing for a seasoned marksman to do. As a hunter Cody killed many buffalo from horseback, but in most cases he was within a few feet of his victim—he merely had to point and pull the trigger. When questioned about his Indian fighting he was frank and modest about the problems of shooting from horseback while traveling fast. When racing horsemen shot at one another, he admitted, the normal result was that nobody hit anything.

Don Russell and others have pointed out that during the wasteful 1867–1868 plains campaign scouts were hired to *find* Indians, not fight them—the army's one purpose was to fight them. Sometimes Cody could locate Indians but he readily acknowledged that Native

American scouts were far better trackers than he ever became. It was the Pawnee scouts working with Major Frank North who found Tall Bull's camp, in the Battle of Summit Springs.

In general, all across the West and Southwest, Native American scouts were usually called in when there was serious tracking to do—in some cases they did serious fighting, too. General Crook's Crow and Shoshoni scouts fought heroically at the Battle of the Rosebud. These scouts, witnesses thought, kept that battle a narrow defeat for Crook, rather than an absolute rout. In the Southwest particularly the Apache scouts were invaluable. Without them Geronimo might still be out.

Strategically the 1867–1868 campaign amounted to very little. General Hancock finally turned his immense command around and lumbered home. Custer's attack on the Washita was the one major battle of the campaign, and it was ill-directed.

I will look a little later at the Battle of Summit Springs, which was not really a major engagement. It's of interest here because it was the first occasion when Cody claimed a kill he probably hadn't made—the same was to occur, under equally debatable circumstances, in the conflict with Yellow Hair.

Sheridan and Carr were, however, right to praise Cody for his willingness to take big risks in order to move (dubious) intelligence from one fort to another. He deserved their praise and earned his $100 bonus. Being a scout and courier happened to be the only military work Cody could perform creditably. As a courier, however dangerous the country, he was once again on his own, enjoying the real if dangerous freedom of the plainsman. He was not afraid to stake his life on his horsemanship, either.

In national terms he may not really have been a *great* scout. He could not claim to have traveled the great reach of territory that Kit Carson, Jedediah Smith (dead before Cody was born), or the Delaware scout Black Beaver all mastered. But he was a better horseman than any of the above—it is entirely fitting that in the poster art created for his shows he is nearly always on horseback. It was on horseback that he looked most like himself—as I have said elsewhere, it is hard to overestimate how far a man can go in America if he looks good on a horse.

He seems never to have lost his skill with horses. Near the end of his life a show horse reared and fell over backwards with him. This is a much dreaded occurrence that has killed many cowboys and not a few rodeo hands. (Such a death occurs in the second volume of my *Lonesome Dove* tetralogy.) But Cody eluded the falling horse, at the cost of a slight injury to his leg. He was still quick enough and horse-savvy enough to mostly get out of the way.

It might be argued, against Helen Cody Wetmore, that her brother William was not quite the last of the great scouts—in that running one would have to at least mention Lonesome Charley Reynolds, the scout Custer sent ninety miles through *very* hostile country to announce that the general had discovered gold in the Black Hills—a place neither general nor scout was supposed to be. Though his horse died and his tongue swelled so from thirst that he couldn't close his mouth, Lonesome Charley made it through to Fort Laramie.

It was General Custer's message about the Black Hills gold that once more, and for the last time, set the high plains ablaze.

12

FOR at least a decade after the Civil War it seemed that every military man west of the Mississippi was either actively pursuing Indians with the intent to kill them or else sitting under a tent painfully hacking out treaties with them, most of which would be broken within weeks, if not sooner.

The writer Alex Shoumatoff has estimated that the U.S. government has broken something like 474 treaties with the native peoples, plenty of which were made and broken during the sixties and seventies of the nineteenth century.

These powwows and treaty-making sessions seem to have frustrated everyone who took part in them, one reason being the language difficulties involved. (Exactly the same difficulties are plaguing coalition soldiers right now in Iraq. Reliable translators from Arabic are proving hard to find.) Few Native American leaders spoke much English, and even fewer of the military negotiators spoke more than a few words of any native language, the consequence being that after a powwow both sides went home without really understanding what they had agreed to. And in any case the government abided by these treaties only to the extent that was convenient.

One especially inconvenient treaty was the one made at the end of the 1860s, giving the Sioux peoples their holy Black Hills in perpetuity, with no whites allowed to be within the sacred area.

General Custer's discovery of gold in these same Black Hills caused one of the most abrupt about-faces in the shameful history of our treaty making and breaking. Perpetuity turned out to be less than five years, after which the greedy Americans tried to buy the land they had so recently surrendered.

General Crook, no fool, advised the Indians to take the money, since nothing could be more obvious than that the whites would anyway soon be taking the land.

The most dramatic years of plains warfare were from 1867 to 1877, that is, from the launching of the Hancock expedition to the surrender of Crazy Horse in May of 1877. Many treaties were made during this decade, mainly because the army did not yet have the manpower to simply overrun the Indians.

Buffalo Bill Cody was in the neighborhood of some of these powwows but the solemnities of oratory and negotiation seem to have held little appeal for him, though later he would do a fair amount of powwowing when he began to hire Indians for his Wild West shows.

Without anyone at first exactly being aware of it, show business began to slyly extend itself out into prairie life. In the beginning this took the form of scouts with colorful monikers, names that might look good on posters or marquees. Besides the guide-turned-showman Texas Jack Omohundro, there were at least two other Texas Jacks, one of whom was hung in Oklahoma for a variety of crimes. There was also a multiplicity of California Joes and, of course, a veritable plethora of Buffalo Bills.

In 1911 or thereabouts Cody was taken to task by a retired hunter named William Mathewson, who insisted that he was the first to be called Buffalo Bill, and that Cody knew it. Cody probably didn't know it but he cheerfully agreed that he had not been the first hunter to be called Buffalo Bill. Later he met Mathewson, saw that he was down on his luck, helped him recover a cherished rifle he had been forced to sell, and quietly settled some of his debts. He and Will Mathewson became good friends.

This was the Cody people loved—many similar stories exist.

One of the first organized showbiz buffalo hunts seems to have occurred somewhere east of Sheridan, Kansas. The hunt featured two Buffalo Bills, Cody and a part-Cheyenne hunter named William

Comstock, who occasionally found himself on the wrong side of the law.

Some doubt that this first show hunt ever took place; the best evidence seems to be archaeological, in the form of a dump containing many beer and champagne bottles. The biographer Courtney Ryley Cooper had a poster advertising the contest, but its authenticity is questionable. A special train holding one hundred spectators chugged out from St. Louis to watch the shooting. Cody claimed to have shot sixty-nine buffalo that day, to Comstock's forty-six. As an additional nicety, which anticipated the showman that he soon would be, Cody managed to kill the final buffalo of the day right in front of the ladies, some of whom may have fainted. Louisa Cody says that the hunt did happen.

Soon after this event or nonevent Cody was part of a group sent to round up deserters from General Hancock's big force. Some of the deserters may simply have been soldiers who got hopelessly lost. Theodore David, a reporter for *Harper's Weekly*, happened to be along on this strange excursion, and it was Wild Bill Hickok, not Buffalo Bill Cody, whose dandyism most stirred the reporter's ire:

> . . . in his usual array Wild Bill could have gained unquestioned admittance to the floor of most fancy dress balls of metropolitan cities. When we ordinary mortals were hustling for a clean pair of socks, as prospective limit of change in wearing apparel, I have seen Wild Bill appear in an immaculate boiled shirt, with collar and cuffs to match—a sleeveless Zouave jacket of startling scarlet, slashed with black velvet . . . the French calfskin . . . boots fitted admirably and were polished as if the individual wearing them had recently vacated an Italian's throne on a sidestreet near Broadway . . . the long wavey hair that fell in masses from a convenient sombrero, was glossy from a recent anointment of some heavily perfumed mixture.

Bill Cody probably read that description of his old friend and learned from it. As much as Hickok he wanted to impress and usually managed to display a casual elegance that, on closer inspection, may not have been so casual—but he never quite slipped over to full dandyism, in the manner of his friend. The reason he didn't was because he had still to sell himself as a workingman of the West, a humble scout, a man who might have to take a hand and drive a stagecoach at any time.

Wild Bill Hickok may have learned from Cody too. One of his bolder experiments, before he made that fatal trip to Deadwood, was to organize that buffalo shoot at Niagara Falls.

13

BEFORE plunging into the dense ambiguities of Cody's two most controversial Indian fights—the Battle of Summit Springs and the "duel" with Yellow Hair—it might be well to finish with the white-hunter phase of Buffalo Bill Cody's career. There is also one lesser Indian fight that is worth mentioning because of the strong element of the theatrical that is apt to be present in any anecdote in which Bill Cody actually claims to have killed an Indian.

In this case, while in pursuit of horse thieves, Cody claims to have killed two Indians with one shot—not impossible, since the two were fleeing on the same horse. This action occurred near the North Platte. Cody then claims that he took the two Indians' warbonnets and gave them to the daughters of General Augur. Warbonnets on men, so surprised that they had to flee on the same horse? Warbonnets, when the Indians were merely out to steal horses? Of course, assuming they had their warbonnets with them, Cody *could* have scavenged them from the raiders' camp.

I raise the question because this is by no means the last time warbonnets occur in Cody's narrative. From here on out virtually every Indian he pursues or claims to have killed is equipped with a warbonnet—though it is usually thought that warbonnets, expensive to produce, might mostly be reserved for formal or ceremonial occasions, such as powwows or ritual dances.

We will keep our eye on warbonnets as we proceed through the final years of Cody's career as a scout.

Later, it seems, there was disagreement as to which general should reap the glory for this chase with horse thieves. What comes clear in the debate is that some military had become acutely jealous of William F. Cody, who was now widely thought of as Sheridan's pet.

With the exception of the grand duke Alexis, most of the hunt organizing Cody did was for rich and influential men who happened to be cronies of Phil Sheridan. James Gordon Bennett of the *New York Herald* was among them, as well as at least two members of the prominent Jerome family, the family which produced the famous Jenny Jerome, Winston Churchill's mother. Bennett was almost as quick as Buntline to recognize Cody's high marketability—it was not long before Cody was summoned to New York, where he was feted by the famous editor and others.

Meanwhile more than one train carload of bankers, financiers, and magnates of various stripes came to Kansas to be stimulated for a day or two while eating buffalo ribs, drinking a lot of champagne, and occasionally shooting off guns.

It might be noted that these mostly half-assed American sportsmen had been preceded on the teeming hunting grounds of the West by several serious hunters from Europe—in particular, from England. The Scotsman William Drummond Stewart hoped to start a large game park in Scotland filled with Western animals. Even before Stewart, Prince Maximilian zu Wied-Neuwied had been up the Missouri, hunting for science rather than for sport. Drummond Stewart took the artist Alfred Jacob Miller with him; the prince of Wied had taken Karl Bodmer; and the enterprising George Catlin took himself: he headed upriver in 1832 on the first steamboat that went. It's because of Miller that we know what the mountain men looked like, while both Catlin and Bodmer left us vivid portraits of many members of the Missouri River tribes in their years of glory, before smallpox and other white man's diseases began to decimate them.

The earl of Dunraven always wanted to establish a large game park, but his was to be in America, not England. He acquired some sixty thousand acres of Colorado, in the Estes Park region, for this purpose, but before the game could be protected the Indians had to agree to stop eating it—the earl's diplomacy was not equal to this task.

Cody himself guided Sir John Watts Garland, an Englishman who liked hunting so much that he established a line of hunting camps, complete with dogs and keepers, to which he returned every year to refresh himself with a little shooting. Sir John seemed less interested in buffalo than in elk, an animal that took some careful stalking.

Some of the English were the opposite of conservationists: they came for slaughter and more slaughter. A fittingly named Englishman, St. George Gore, is said to have killed at least twenty-five hundred buffalo, to the disgust of Jim Bridger and others.

Cody also briefly guided the famous pioneering paleontologist Othniel Charles Marsh, who ventured out often from his citadel at Yale.

The duck hunt recently enjoyed by Vice President Cheney and Supreme Court Justice Antonin Scalia is exactly the sort of well-planned excursion that Cody was good at managing. Shouldn't busy and prominent men be allowed to shoot guns and drink whiskey in their own company now and then?

As Don Russell points out, royals of any stamp were rare in America in the nineteenth century. When one promised to show up—even if the royal was only a third son, as was the case with the grand duke Alexis, not exactly the sharpest knife in the Romanov drawer—big attention needed to be paid, and America was eager to pay it. The Russian royal fleet took a long time getting across the pond, but eventually, in the fall of 1871, it showed up.

Cody was at this time still chief of scouts of the Fifth Cavalry, which was about to depart for Arizona to deal with the elusive and troublesome Apaches; but a letter from General Sheridan arrived just in time to keep Cody from leaving. He was to find buffalo for the grand duke—a promising hunting site some forty miles west of Fort McPherson was soon selected, and what came to be called Camp Alexis was hastily constructed.

Cody was probably pleased with being awarded this plum, but

he may have been less pleased when he found out that Alexis was particularly eager to see some wild Indians while he was on this hunt.

The royal hunt was to take place early in 1872, a time when it would not have been hard to find plenty of wild Indians—the catch was that they might just want to behave like what they were, *wild* Indians. The war for the great plains was still very much a going thing: Fetterman and his eighty men had been wiped out only a few years before the grand duke's visit, and one of the duke's hunting partners, George Armstrong Custer, would be wiped out a few years after their hunt. Every army officer knew that if invited to do a war dance, the young braves might forget that they were actors and do some fine scalping while they had the chance.

Since nobody wanted to say no to a grand duke, a chief had to be chosen and asked if he and some of his warriors would mind providing some entertainment for this important person from across the seas.

The military powers decided on Spotted Tail, the more or less cooperative leader of the Brulé Sioux. Spotted Tail had been to Washington and was well aware of how the cookie was likely to crumble, where his people were concerned. He was at the time hunting buffalo on the Republican River, where Cody, traveling alone, found him and persuaded him to oblige General Sheridan, if it wouldn't be too much trouble.

It wasn't too much trouble. Spotted Tail (who was eventually killed by one of his own people) showed up right on time and put on a splendid show—very probably it was this event that convinced Cody it would not be impossible to use Indians in the Wild West shows. The war dance was most effective and a particularly skilled hunter named Two Lances much pleased the grand duke by shooting an arrow completely through a running buffalo.

General Custer, as was his wont, flirted with one of Spotted Tail's comely daughters, neither the first nor the last flirtation Custer pursued with good-looking native women.

Matthew Brady, pioneering photojournalist, showed up and took everybody's picture.

The grand duke Alexis, a rather stolid youth, had a passionate

interest in firearms but an almost total absence of skill when it came
to using them. Alexis had visited the Smith & Wesson factory on his
way west—he was eager to drop a buffalo with one of his new pistols
and proceeded to empty two six-shooters at a buffalo standing some
twenty feet away; the twelve bullets went somewhere, but the buffalo
was unfazed.

Reluctantly the grand duke gave up the revolver but allowed
Cody to loan him his famous buffalo rifle, Lucretia Borgia (a breech-
loading Springfield), as well as his best buffalo horse, Buckskin Joe,
which swiftly carried the grand duke to within a yard or two of a
buffalo. Lucretia Borgia spoke and the buffalo fell over, much to the
relief of everyone involved. Champagne flowed, as it was to do later
in the day when the grand duke brought down a buffalo cow. On the
way back to camp Cody treated the grand duke to a stagecoach ride,
another proto-act which later proved popular in London, where
Cody once got four kings into the Deadwood stage.

The grand duke gave Cody a fur coat and some cuff links—but
the main thing he gave him was something to think about. The hunt
was just one more rich man's frolic, but the fact that the Indians had
agreed to provide entertainment, and *had* provided entertainment,
was, at the time, a singular thing. Cody may not have immediately
connected it with his own future, but he didn't forget it, either.
Within a decade's time some of the Indians who had entertained the
grand duke Alexis found that they had nothing better to do than to
let Pahaska put them in a show.

Cody himself, once the grand duke departed, found that his
management of this tame hunt reaped a huge amount of publicity,
all of it favorable to himself. With the Fifth Cavalry gone west there
was not much for him to do, so he accepted James Gordon Bennett's
invitation and went to New York, after which visit—though he continued to go back to the plains—his life was never to be quite the
same.

14

I T is perhaps best to step back a year from these high-profile hunts to the somewhat inconclusive prairie campaigns of 1869–1870, spin-offs to General Hancock's expensive but largely futile expedition. Cody was still chief of scouts of the Fifth Cavalry, but at the reduced pay of $75 a month; he was briefly stationed at Fort Lyon in eastern Colorado. It was to Fort Lyon that Black Kettle carried his wounded wife after the Sand Creek Massacre. There were plenty of Indians to fight—during one brief skirmish Cody received one of his very rare wounds: his hat was shot off and his scalp creased, producing a heavy blood flow. Cody kept on fighting, a fact that impressed General Carr so much that he awarded him a bonus of $100.

The so-called Battle of Summit Springs, in which the Cheyenne leader Tall Bull and a number of his dog soldiers were apparently killed, was perhaps the most confusing of Cody's many confusing fracasses. As many as twenty versions of this conflict exist, half of those emanating, over a period of some sixty years, from one informant—Luther North, brother of Major Frank North, who may or may not have killed Tall Bull himself. At the time of the battle Frank North was the organizer and leader of a group of Pawnee scouts. (Later Frank North was to partner with Cody, both in the cattle business and the Wild West shows.)

The confusions produced by this battle result from the fact that the trail along which the cavalry was pursuing the main band of Cheyenne split at some point. Cody and some of the troop proceeded along what seemed to be the main trail and eventually arrived at the

Cheyennes' main camp, while Frank North, his brother, and some of the Pawnee scouts followed a smaller trail and eventually encountered a small force of Indians in a ravine. One of these Indians may have been Tall Bull. Frank North tricked this Indian into showing his head, at which moment he shot him. Only later, after talking with the Pawnee scouts, did he conclude that the dead Indian was Tall Bull.

Cody's version, appearing in various editions of his autobiography, is at first glance simpler. As battle raged in the large village Cody saw an Indian on a magnificent bay horse; he promptly shot the Indian and claimed the horse, which later proved the swiftest in all Nebraska, winning Cody many races. In Luther North's version, or one of them, this splendid horse is cream-colored; in even later versions the horse becomes a gray. One version mentions that the horse had received a stab wound.

Then, in the Cody version, the dead Indian's wife begins to wail and he learns that he has killed her husband, Tall Bull. In the course of the battle this same woman had herself dispatched one of the two white captives the troop had been hoping to rescue. The victim was a Mrs. Alderdice, brained with a tomahawk and buried at the scene. The other captive, a Mrs. Weichel, though wounded, survived the battle and married the hospital orderly who tended her at Fort Sedgwick.

Cody's mandate, on this adventure, was to find the Indians, and with the help of the able Pawnee scouts, he did find them. Whether he had any idea who Tall Bull was is not clear: he shot an Indian because he wanted his horse—for the time being the matter of Tall Bull did not interest him.

Luther North, however, continued to be mildly obsessed with the killing of Tall Bull until at least 1929, when he issued the last of his nearly innumerable versions. He became obsessed with the need to correct the record and establish that his own brother, Frank North, had killed this important chief.

At first Frank North himself was no more invested than Cody in the killing of Tall Bull. He had tricked an Indian who was hiding in a ravine. The Indian fell dead. North, like Cody, may not have considered Tall Bull to be particularly important.

When asked by his importunate brother Luther why he didn't correct the record, Frank North merely pointed out that Cody was in show business whereas he wasn't.

Much later, perhaps because his brother wouldn't let the matter fade, Frank North did develop a bias against Cody over the matter of Tall Bull. George Bird Grinnell, author of *The Fighting Cheyenne*, accepted Luther North's version, or one of them, and included it in his book. But Frank North's annoyance was temporary—for the rest of his life he worked with Cody amiably enough.

In Cody's many versions of the conflict, the battle itself tends to slide around. At first Cody claimed he shot Tall Bull off the handsome bay from a distance of about thirty feet; this grew, in time, to "fully four hundred yards," and again, a warbonnet finds its way into the story. It seems that in Cody's memory of the old West the major Indians were as clothes conscious as he was himself. They all seemed to wear their warbonnets at all times, even at breakfast.*

The Tall Bull business became even more confusing when one of the many reprints of Cody's book was in press. The copy the printer was working from proved to be missing several pages—unfortunately the pages had to do with the Battle of Summit Springs. Cody was in England when this problem was discovered. All the printer had to go on was an illustration from an earlier edition of the book. The illustration was called *The Killing of Tall Bull*. On his own initiative the printer scribbled in his version of what the Battle of Summit Springs must have been like. In his version the body count rises from fifty-two (itself probably an exaggeration) to six hundred. The book this version appears in is called *The Story of the Wild West*. Cody had little interest in reading about these old battles and was probably unaware of the vastly inflated body count. Whether he killed Tall Bull or not never greatly interested him. His primary job had been to find the Indians, and he found them, acquiring, as a bonus, an excellent racehorse (bay, cream-colored, or gray as it may be). Also he had helped free one of the two female captives. Most scholars agree that Tall Bull was killed that day, but who killed him will probably remain in dispute.

* The artist Charles Schreyvogel has a painting called *The Summit Spring's Rescue 1869* in which Cody is shown shooting an Indian warrior who killed Mrs. Alderdice. Paul Andrew Hutton, in his excellent study *Phil Sheridan and His Army*, says that Cody took no part in the rescue of the captives but believes that he did kill Tall Bull.

15

BILL CODY'S interests were eclectic. He was able to appreciate many things, among them the city of New York, about which he was soon as enthusiastic as he had been about the cool air and large freedoms of the prairies. He was a handsome addition to the great metropolitan scene—in no time he was receiving so many invitations that he got mixed up and missed an important dinner hosted by James Gordon Bennett.

One person he got little help from on this visit was Ned Buntline, who had troubles of his own, chief among them bigamy. Buntline was living with a fourth wife, while remaining imperfectly divorced from the first three, a costly situation in more ways than one.

The only thing Buffalo Bill didn't like on this visit to New York was his own performance in *Buffalo Bill: King of the Border Men*, a role he found so terrifying that the few words he managed to mumble could not even be heard by the orchestra leader, a few feet away. Fortunately General Sheridan soon interrupted this period of internal stage fright; Cody was summoned back to Fort McPherson so abruptly that he forgot his trunk and was forced to plunge right into an Indian fight while still in evening dress—in my view an unlikely story, since there were not a few haberdasheries between New York City and Fort McPherson, in Nebraska.

According to Cody the reason the general wanted him back in such a hurry was an outbreak of horse thieves. Cody claims that he rode right up beside an Indian on a stolen horse and shot him in the head, a big deviation from his usual practice of aiming for the horse and not the man.

Not much that Cody said about this particular period, when he was trying to learn to lead a double life, now on the plains and now on the stage, can be taken literally. Much telescoping and probably much invention was involved. Cody thought the skirmish in which he shot the Indian in the head to be of little account, but, bizarrely, he got the Congressional Medal of Honor for it anyway, although the award was rescinded in 1916 since Cody had apparently been a civilian at the time of this fight.

Meanwhile, back in North Platte, Lulu was delivered of Orra Maude, their third child. The earl of Dunraven asked Cody to guide him on a hunt but Cody turned this attractive chore over to Texas Jack Omohundro, with whom he often worked.

Cody then ran for the state legislature and was elected, but charges of hanky-panky were raised and he never took his disputed seat. Instead, once Texas Jack was free the two of them went to Chicago and were soon on the stage. Cody even began to lose his stage fright—for the next ten years Cody would be back and forth between prairie and stage. Ned Buntline escaped all four of his wives and showed up in Chicago, where he first distinguished himself by taking part in an anti-German riot. Though he scribbled off many terrible plays both Cody and Omohundro kept him at arm's length. Wild Bill Hickok tried the stage with Cody a few times but the stage lighting bothered his weak eyes; the same poor eyesight caused him to fire his blank bullets too close to the bare legs of the stage Indians, resulting in painful powder burns. It seems to me, contra Evan Connell, that Hickok, rather than Cody, was the real mixture of thespian and assassin. Hickok's myopia suggests that in real fights his victims must have stood very close to hand. This was clearly the case in his famous fight with the McCandles brothers. One thing Cody and Hickok had in common was that their public images soon eclipsed anything resembling reality. They became legends in their own time, which was lucky in the case of the rising young showman Bill Cody, but was not so lucky in the case of James Butler Hickok.

16

THE death, in June of 1876, of General George Armstrong Custer and some 250 men of the famed Seventh Cavalry was a shock to the nation comparable in some ways to Pearl Harbor or 9/11. The scale may have been much smaller but the shock was still tremendous; like 9/11 the massacre at the Little Bighorn was completely unexpected. In fact, in his report for 1875, the commissioner for Indian Affairs stated that it was no longer probable that even five hundred belligerent warriors could ever again be mustered for a fight.

Obviously military intelligence was as imperfect in 1875 as it is today, since the very next summer an estimated ten thousand Indians assembled near the Little Bighorn, and, as Custer was shortly to discover, they were quite belligerent.

Once the shock had been absorbed by a confused nation, there arose, as was inevitable, a cry for punishment, but punishment was never to be conclusively administered because the ten thousand hostile tribespeople simply melted away into the prairies and the hills. The figure mentioned by the commissioner in his 1875 Report—five hundred—would now, indeed, have been hard to locate.

Cody had been fulfilling theatrical obligations in the East; he continued to fulfill them even though griefstricken by the death of his son, Kit Carson Cody. He ended his run with a benefit performance in Wilmington, Delaware, about two weeks before the Custer massacre and was already on his way west when the massacre occurred. Apparently the army intended to send Cody to scout for General George Crook, who was about to fight the taxing battle of the Rosebud, a week before the Little Bighorn.

Cody didn't immediately make it to the Rosebud, although Crook could certainly have used him. Instead Cody joined his old company, the Fifth Cavalry, then commanded by General Merritt— the Fifth was generally charged with keeping peace at the populous Red Cloud agency, the one place where five hundred ready-and-willing warriors might have been found. The Red Cloud agency was northeast of Fort Laramie, across the Platte from Fort Robinson, where Crazy Horse would eventually be killed. By the time Cody reached his company it was the middle of July, about two weeks after the massacre.

Frightened, fearful of reprisals, lots of Indians did leave the Red Cloud agency during this confusing period, and neither General Merritt nor anyone else knew quite what to do about them.

On the night of July 16, the Fifth Cavalry camped near Hat Creek, sometimes called Warbonnet Creek, just northwest of the Red Cloud agency. On the morning of the seventeenth, Cody was out at dawn and he soon noted signs of restlessness in the big Cheyenne camp nearby. He approached a young signalman, Chris Madsen, and told him to signal General Merritt that the Cheyenne seemed to be preparing to move.

In fact a portion of the big Cheyenne party split off, in the hopes of intercepting two military messengers who were coming toward General Merritt's camp, unaware of how much trouble they were about to find themselves in. Cody and a number of cavalrymen hurried to cut off the Cheyenne who were trying to cut off the messengers. Cody seems to have been dressed in a black velvet suit at the time, though upon reaching the bivouac he had been wearing immaculate white buckskins.

Here is Cody's version—many times repeated and reenacted but not really embellished—of his "duel" with Wey-o-hei, or Yellow Hair (called Yellow Hand by Cody and almost everyone else):

We were about half a mile from General Merritt, and the Indians whom we were chasing suddenly turned on us, and another lively skirmish took place. One of the Indians, who was handsomely decorated with all the ornaments usually worn by a war chief when engaged in a fight, sang out to me in his own tongue: I know you, Pa-he-haska; if you want to fight come ahead and fight me.

The chief was riding his horse back and forth in front of his men, as if to banter me, and I concluded to accept the challenge. I galloped toward him for about fifty yards and he advanced to me about fifty yards, the same distance, both of us riding at full speed, and when we were only about thirty yards apart, I raised my rifle and fired; his horse fell to the ground, having been killed by my bullet.

At almost the same instant my own horse went down, he having stepped into a hole. The fall did not hurt me much and I instantly sprang to my feet. The Indian had also recovered himself, and we were both on foot, not twenty yards apart. We fired at each other simultaneously. My usual luck did not desert me, for his bullet missed me while mine struck him in the breast. He reeled and fell, but before he had fairly touched the ground I was upon him, knife in hand, and had driven the keen-edged weapon to the hilt in his heart. Jerking his warbonnet off, I scientifically scalped him in about five seconds . . .

The whole affair from beginning to end occupied but very little time.

As the soldiers came up I swung the Indian chieftain's top knot and bonnet into the air and shouted: the first scalp for Custer!

Some of the other Cheyenne, seeing that Cody was alone, charged down at him, but the quick-thinking General Merritt already had reinforcements on the way, and anyhow, Cody had some cavalry with him when he set out to cut off the Cheyenne.

The novelist, mountaineer, military man, and longtime friend of Henry Adams, Clarence King, happened to be with the Fifth Cavalry that morning and was deeply impressed—intoxicated, even—with the glamour of the fighting Cheyenne. He may also have been literally intoxicated, which could have caused his enthusiasm for native color to rise to a fever pitch:

> Savage warfare was never more beautiful than in you. On you come, your swift, agile ponies swinging down the winding ravine, the rising sun shining on your trailing warbonnets, on silver armlets, necklace, gorget; on brilliant painted shield and beaded leggin; on naked body and fearless face, stained most vivid vermilion. On you come, lance and rifle, pennon and feather glistening in the rare morning light, swaying in the wild grace of your peerless horsemanship; nearer, till I mark the very ornament on your leader's shield.

Signalman Madsen probably had the best view of the Cody and Wey-o-hei fight, a view rather less Knights of the Round Table than Cody's own:

> Cody was riding a little in advance of his party and one of the Indians was preceding his group. I was standing on the butte where I had been stationed. It was some distance from the place where they met but I had an unobstructed view of all that happened. Through the powerful telescope furnished by the Signal Department the men did not appear to be more than 50 feet from me. From the manner in which both parties acted it was certain that both were surprised. Cody and the leading Indians appeared to be the only ones who did not become excited. The instant they were face to face their guns fired. It seemed almost like one shot. There was no conversation, no preliminary agreement as has been stated in some novels written by romantic scribes.
>
> They met by accident and fired the minute they faced each other. Cody's bullet went through the Indian's leg and killed his pinto pony. The Indian's bullet went wild. Cody's horse stepped in a prairie dog hole and stumbled but was up in a moment. Cody jumped clear of his mount. Kneel-

ing, he took deliberate aim and fired the second shot. An instant before Cody fired the Indian fired at him but missed. Cody's bullet went through the Indian's head and ended the battle. Cody went over to the fallen warrior Indian and neatly removed his scalp while the other soldiers gave chase to the Indian's companions. There is no doubt about it, Buffalo Bill scalped this Indian who, it turned out, was a Cheyenne sub-chief called Yellow Hair.

Signalman Madsen, unlike Cody and everybody else, actually got Yellow Hair's name right. The confident Madsen later took the trouble to poke no less than twenty-eight holes in Clarence King's account of the skirmish. Yet another signalman, Sergeant John Powers, who was riding with a small wagon train at the time, further deromanticized Cody's "duel" with Yellow Hair in a report which appeared in the *Ellis County Star*, a paper which thoroughly scooped both the *New York Herald* and the *Chicago Times* on this occasion. Here is Sergeant Powers's version:

> Three or four Indians started out on a run to cut off the dispatch bearers. They had not seen the command and were not aware that we were in the vicinity; but Bill Cody and his scouts were watching them . . . He then got around the Indians and when he felt sure of the couriers Cody raised up behind a little hill and shot the pony of one of the redskins. Then starting after his victim he soon had him killed and his scalp off . . .
>
> The Indian killed by Buffalo Bill proved to be Yellow Hand, sub–war chief of the Southern Cheyenne.

The *New York Herald* asked Cody for a report on the incident and Cody persuaded King to file one—it was this account that Signalman Madsen poked twenty-eight holes in. When Clarence King was shown the clipping some fifty years later he disclaimed it.

Cody himself wrote Lulu the day after the fight, enclosing Yellow Hair's scalp, warbonnet, whip, and guns. The Codys were then living in Buffalo, and Cody wanted these spoils of war exhibited in a local department store, to help advertise a Western melodrama he was committed to. These have long since migrated to the Cody museum in Cody, Wyoming. The "duel" aspects of the encounter have since grown in the telling, chiefly through elaborations in Cody's sister's books.

As the years passed several people challenged Cody's claim to have killed Yellow Hair. One claim that has at least vague plausibility was made by the ubiquitous scout Baptiste "Little Bat" Garnier, a well-traveled plainsman who at one time was a friend of Crazy Horse. Little Bat was present that day but didn't claim the kill himself; it was claimed for him by his son, Johnny Bat, who said that Cody had actually been challenged to a knife fight by Yellow Hair and was prepared to take up the challenge. Little Bat, being of the opinion that Cody would swiftly be cut to ribbons, got off his horse and shot the Indian.

A grislier variant of this claim surfaced in 1927—indeed, several of the wilder accounts did not appear until the late twenties, probably because by this time Cody had made a movie about his duel with Yellow Hair—it was called *Indian Wars*. The grisly version is that Little Bat had actually killed Yellow Hair a couple of days before at a buffalo wallow and had simply let him lie. Later, hearing that Cody wanted a scalp, Little Bat led Cody to the buffalo wallow and Cody then took the somewhat fragrant trophy—this strikes me as unlikely.

In 1929 Herbert Cody Blake, who sounds like a disgruntled relative, published an anti-Cody pamphlet called *Blake's Western Stories,* in which five soldiers claiming to be present that day all testify that Cody did *not* kill Yellow Hair. Blake's is a debunking polemic and the testimony came fifty-two years after the event.

Around this time (the twenties) several common soldiers showed up, all insisting that they had killed Yellow Hair. Most of these belated claimants do not appear in army registers; they seem to have just convinced themselves, after much brooding, that they probably killed the famous Indian.

Another report from the twenties mentions that Yellow Hair's wife showed up at headquarters and cut off a finger, to show her distress.

In fact Yellow Hair had *not* been a famous Indian—he became famous with his death. Both Madsen and Powers identify him as a subchief. He seems merely to have been an alert lookout who quickly saw a chance to cut off the two messengers.

The composer and diarist Ned Rorem remarks somewhere that all life is really *Rashomon*—a matter, that is, of individual point of view. Most of Bill Cody's encounters with Indians demonstrate this quality. Cody wrote his autobiography, three years after his "duel," to energize his theatrical career. Naturally he and his ghostwriter splashed in as much color as possible.

By his own account he and Yellow Hair were more than one hundred yards apart when the Cheyenne "sang out" his challenge. He would have had to sing it pretty loud for Cody to hear it—Cody, of course, did not speak Cheyenne nor Yellow Hair English. Besides, Yellow Hair knew that there was a large company of soldiers near at hand. It is extremely unlikely that he would have put himself in jeopardy to enjoy some kind of duel with Bill Cody, whom he may not even have recognized, despite the latter's velvet suit.

I see no reason to doubt the sober testimony of the two signalmen, Madsen and Powers; both had a good view and neither had any axe to grind. Some discrepancies usually pop up in battle reports. Cody shot Yellow Hair in the leg yet the bullet hit his horse in the head, killing him. Some say both men's first shot missed. The claim that Cody took advantage of a hill or rise to conceal himself makes sense. Cody had always been prudent. Yellow Hair may have slipped, for a time, into a shallow ravine. Each would have naturally used whatever topographical advantage they could find. That Cody, once unhorsed, went down on one knee and took deliberate aim is convincing—he often complained about the difficulty of making precise shots from moving horses. It was characteristic of him to shoot the horse first—he did this some half a dozen times. Certainly he was not fool enough to allow himself to be drawn into a knife fight, and of course he was aware that Yellow Hair had massive reinforcements at hand: the charging Cheyenne Clarence King was so impressed with.

Neither signalman mentions Cody stabbing the Indian—merely scalping him.

General Merritt was on top of the situation and sent Cody rapid backup.

Much later, when the regimental history was compiled, here's the summing up: "William F. Cody, the favorite scout of the regiment, was conspicuous in the affair of the morning, having killed in hand-to-hand conflict Yellow Hand, a prominent Cheyenne chief."

Cody informed Lulu that he had killed the Cheyenne in single-hand fight and mentioned that he would forward the warbonnet and the rest as soon as he reached Fort Laramie. He also said she would be reading about it in the papers.

The eight hundred Cheyenne, whatever they thought of the hand-to-hand conflict, allowed themselves to be conducted back to the Red Cloud agency, where they washed off their war paint and put away their warbonnets. Don Russell remarks that the Cheyenne were pretty impressed with Cody—probably because of the suit rather than the fight. Cody too was friendly. It was no doubt in the back of his mind that he might need some of these Indians someday.

The exploit made the *New York Herald* on July 23, 1876. It was perhaps the most newsworthy report to come out of the West for the duration of the rambling, rumbling military effort to punish the northern tribes for Custer's spectacular defeat.

An odd consequence of it was that Cody's sister Josephine married Big Bat Pourriere—he was called Big Bat to distinguish him from Little Bat Garnier.

On August 2 this death-filled summer claimed one more well-known star: Wild Bill Hickok was murdered in Deadwood while playing cards.

17

THE Fifth Cavalry did finally join up with General George Crook—the Gray Fox, to the Indians—and Cody became chief of scouts with the Bighorn and Yellowstone expeditions. Crook, notoriously, was a no-frills general. His cooking equipment consisted of a cup and a stick. In the cup he boiled his coffee; on the stick he cooked his bacon. His attire was of the plainest. The contrast with General Terry's large, beautifully equipped company became evident a little later, once the two armies joined up. Cody, no opponent of luxury, was nonetheless made a little uneasy by the cumbersome nature of Terry's equipage. It seemed unlikely they would catch the fleet Sioux or the equally fleet Cheyenne while traveling so heavy. General Crook probably thought the same, but he was polite to Terry, by all accounts a genial and likable man.

This top-heavy command was soon made even more top-heavy by the arrival of General Nelson A. Miles. Exactly what this massive force supposed it was doing is not entirely clear, although there is a huge literature that follows the various generals on an almost day-to-day basis. Mainly it was supposed to prevent the Indians who were responsible for the massacre from getting away, although it was of course clear to even the dullest military man that they had already gotten away.

Cody, as chief of scouts, loped around hither and thither but found no Indians. The conflict with Yellow Hair had occurred in the middle of July—by the middle of August Cody was tired of this aimless proceeding. In late August he resigned and headed downriver on the steamer *Yellowstone*, but he soon ran into his old partner Texas Jack Omohundro, who was headed upriver with dispatches for various and sundry. Since Cody was not particularly eager to get home to Lulu and the children, he decided to hang around with Texas Jack.

Then General Whistler and General Terry convinced themselves that the woods near the Yellowstone River were crawling with savages—this was mostly paranoia, but it meant that Cody's skills as a courier were once more, and for the last time, in demand. He made several dangerous rides, carrying various dispatches. Once, dozing in a ravine, he was nearly overrun by some thirty Indians who were chasing buffalo. They made several kills and butchered the animals on the spot, but did not discover Cody, who hid until nightfall and then made a wide swing around them.

For this last flurry of scouting Cody was paid $200, much the largest sum he had ever earned as a scout. Once he resigned for a second time, he took the steamer *Far West* as far as Bismarck, and then went home to Rochester by train.

Had he so chosen, Cody could have hung on one more year as a scout. In the winter of 1877 Ranald Mackenzie relentlessly pursued Dull Knife and his Cheyenne. Both Sitting Bull and Crazy Horse were still out; General Miles pursued them in a generally futile winter campaign. The Indians thought the whites must have gone crazy—no one with any sense fought in winter. Sitting Bull soon took his Hunkpapas to Canada. In May of 1877 Crazy Horse came in, with nine hundred people and two thousand horses. Not long afterward the Nez Perce fled Idaho and made their own race for Canada—they were stopped by General Miles just forty miles short of their goal. Chief Joseph vowed to fight no more forever and in fact was not given the chance. Except for the aberrant breakout at Pine Ridge in 1890, the Plains Indian wars were over.

The only remaining problem was Geronimo and a few of his Apache allies. General Crook tried a second time to straighten out Apache affairs. Crook seemed to like Cody, who was always deferential to generals, and probably would have hired him to locate the renegade Apaches, but Cody expressed no interest. Although he would eventually go to Arizona and build a big hotel at Mountain View, he did not want to follow the Gray Fox into the snakes and boulders of the distant, dusty Apacheria.

When the last of the great scouts stepped off that steamer in Bismarck and transferred to the rails, he had—whether he was aware of it or not—ended a phase of his life. He was thirty years old and had been a scout for fully half that time. The adventures he had had would provide colorful fodder for hundreds of tableaux, playlets, dime novels, and Wild West shows. Cody had an excellent memory for landscape but a poor memory for almost everything else. He became confused about much that he had done, getting dates and distances mixed up and sometimes claiming a deeper involvement than he may actually have had in various little skirmishes. He nevertheless *was* Buffalo Bill Cody, a figure who had held a colorful place on the American frontier. He *had* done a lot, he was bona fide; he didn't get lost and danger didn't deter him.

Though he would never be employed as a scout again, something of what he had done remained part of him to the end. He was a fine horseman—just the way he carried himself on a horse mesmerized audiences.

The former scout who boarded the train to Rochester had forty years to live. Though he bought a ranch, invested in this and that, tried various forms of entrepreneurship, he was essentially in showbiz for the rest of his life.

BOOK TWO

The Troupes

1

THE American theater in the last quarter of the nineteenth century, when Bill Cody turned to it for his livelihood, was a very catch-as-catch-can institution. Actors had begun to realize that they could not book their shows, direct their shows, write their shows, find costumes for their shows—not if they were expected to have energy left to *act* in their shows, though acting was for them the whole point.

Those shadowy figures—advance man, booking agent, and publicist—were clearly needed but had not yet cleanly separated themselves from the actors. Ned Buntline was an all-purpose showman. He performed all the above-mentioned functions—advance man, booking agent, publicist—but he didn't perform any of them very well.

Amateurishness abounded, but Cody and Omohundro and Buntline all realized that some sort of administrative system had to develop if they were to make any kind of consistent money. They could not just flounder helplessly from melodrama to melodrama, hoping things would somehow work out. Audiences were now past the point where they would pay just to see a bunch of tall yokels in buckskins walking around onstage with guns.

Cody had installed his family in Rochester. He returned to them in September of 1876, about two months after he had killed Yellow Hair—an experience which he at once converted into actionable material. The agile Prentiss Ingraham rushed out a dime novel called

The Right Red Hand: Or Buffalo Bill's First Scalp for Custer. This brash effort was quickly converted into a five-act play, a dramatic vehicle which Cody modestly described as being "without head or tail . . . it made no difference which act we commenced the performances . . . It afforded us, however, ample opportunity to give a noisy, rattling gunpowder entertainment and to present a succession of scenes in the great Indian war." The play was first staged in the Rochester Opera House but soon moved on to the Grand Opera in New York City, where Cody tried for a time to exhibit Yellow Hair's scalp and warbonnet to perk the crowd's interest. When the play toured New England he had problems with the clergy and had to withdraw the scalp from the showcase, but he still kept it handy and offered lots of people a look at it. This did not hurt the gate receipts.

Cody's use of Yellow Hair's scalp did not stop there—he showed it to the press at almost every show, a fact which gives a measure of credibility to Little Bat Garnier's assertion that Cody—knowing his time as a scout was nearly over—was really looking to acquire a scalp. His encounter with Yellow Hair was probably a surprise to both men—but Cody was very capable of thinking ahead to a day when a scalp and a warbonnet might come in handy, publicity-wise, particularly if the scalp happened to be the "first scalp for Custer."

There is no evidence that Cody scalped Tall Bull, if it was Tall Bull he killed, or any other of the various Indians who may have fallen to his gun.

In the 1870s what we would now call troupes or even repertory companies were mostly called "combinations." These combinations would need to have a male lead, a female lead, some villains, stooges, maybe an Indian or two, maybe a juggler, and so forth. When Cody returned to the East it seemed that his old friend Texas Jack Omohundro, whom he had recently seen in the Yellowstone country, had got the jump on him when it came to putting together a crowd-pleasing combination.

For one thing Texas Jack, with whom Cody always had amiable relations, had taken the prudent step of marrying his beautiful costar, Giuseppina Morlacchi, always referred to as the "peerless

Morlacchi," a dancer who was also a professional actress, able to handle many roles. She was a very beautiful young woman, one of her claims to fame being that she had introduced the cancan to America. Texas Jack also employed the man who would later become Cody's lifelong press agent, John M. Burke, then an actor known as Arizona John, whose role seemed to have required him to empty his pistol rapidly at every performance.

Cody always had too much raw star power for Texas Jack to compete with, but when it came to organizing a modern theatrical troupe, Texas Jack for a time pulled ahead. He had, for one thing, his charming wife, described by one Chicago critic as "a beautiful Indian maiden with an Italian accent and a weakness for scouts."

Unfortunately, in 1880, just three years after he and Cody had resumed their friendly rivalry, Texas Jack Omohundro suddenly died while performing in Leadville, Colorado. He can be seen in many photographs, in most of which he is standing beside his lovely, diminutive wife and his tall friend Buffalo Bill.

2

As a performer, Bill Cody dealt in broad strokes, one reason his shows turned out to work best in arenas or sports palaces. But even on a small stage, he got better notices than Ned Buntline, whom one harsh critic described as being "simply maundering imbecility. Ludicrous beyond description is Ned Buntline's temperance address in the forest."

Recognizing perhaps that the finer points of acting were, and might always be, beyond him, Cody, at the very beginning of his performing career, immediately announced a farewell tour—the first of many such:

> This will be the last season that Buffalo Bill (W. F. Cody) will travel as a theatrical star. The company he now has is engaged for fifteen months, one of which is to be passed on vacation. The troupe, about the middle of June, will arrive in Omaha, and then they will be transported at the manager's expense to his ranch on the North Platte, where they will be at liberty to do as they please. Toward the end of June they will start for San Francisco and play there for four weeks. Thence through California, Oregon, Nevada, and Utah, back to Omaha, where they will disband, Buffalo Bill going to his ranch, to remain there the rest of his life as a cattle dealer and gentleman farmer. He now has 4,500 head of cattle and hopes to have 10,000 by the close

of next year. He will, therefore, retire from the stage with ample competence.

The farewell tour was in fact an inaugural tour, led by a young actor of thirty-one years, who had no competence to speak of, if by competence he meant money. This same Buffalo Bill Cody would continue to perform for almost exactly forty more years, many times in what he called farewell performances. The final performance, in Chicago in 1916, was more of a rodeo than a Wild West show, leaning heavily on cowboy contests.

What Cody recognized at the outset of his career was that "farewells" always play—many a spectator's eye, over these forty years, would go misty at the thought that they might never see Buffalo Bill again. Cody, like many another impresario, milked farewells for whatever they were worth. His theatrical instincts may have been crude, but they were mainly sound.

It was this instinct which led him, against all advice, to launch a West Coast tour. It was suggested to him that people who actually lived in the West were not likely to respond to these absurd Western melodramas; but Cody's instinct was sharper. He recognized that the westering experience was a source of powerful myth, and that many people who lived in the West might prefer, for an hour or two, the fantasy rather than the reality. Theater, like the movies which followed, wasn't about reason or good sense; it was an *escape* from reason, common sense, and the daily grind. Cody realized this early on; what he offered was a pageant of the past, colorful if not necessarily realistic. The people lapped it up.

Lulu Cody, who stayed for a while in Denver, where Cody's sisters lived, actually accompanied him on much of the West Coast tour, an experience she would not repeat. Probably she went in order to keep an eye on her husband, which meant remaining constantly on the alert. When the troupe finally disbanded in Omaha, all the actresses in the troupe insisted on kissing their Papa Bill good-bye. Cody remembers that the girls were all having a glass or two of beer, so he had a glass or two with them, to be convivial. Cody seldom turned down drink, and had no objection to kissing pretty women.

Lulu, however, had loud objections: she had a fit, bawled him out, and rarely traveled with him after that. As to the kissing, Cody could not understand what Lulu thought could possibly be wrong with it.

> I do not think that most wives would have felt a little angry to know and hear her husband in an adjoining room on Sunday morning, drinking beer and kissing the theatrical girls of his company. I think they would have been rather proud of a husband who had six or seven months work with a party of people who were in his employ, to know and feel that they were on a kindly people footing . . . Not one of them got up and kissed papa goodbye, but all four of them rushed up and kissed papa, their old manager, goodbye . . . Actresses are not narrow-minded people . . . I was just 31 then, just the right age.

I don't know if Lulu Cody saw this long statement, but if she did it no doubt confirmed her worst fears: actresses were not narrow-minded people and her husband was just the right age; besides that he was to stay the right age for most of the rest of his life and was to encounter several actresses, among them Katherine Clemmons, who were even less narrow-minded than the girls of that first troupe.

House receipts for the California tour were very encouraging—one night in San Francisco they pulled in $1,400. Lulu went home to North Platte and saw to the erection of the big house they called Scout's Rest. Cody had proven that Western plays, if anything, did better in the West than in the East. Not long after that, convinced that a few real Indians were essential if he was to keep his productions exciting, he journeyed to the Red Cloud agency and secured the services of a few, a move that was not welcome in Washington—the government considered Indians wards of the state, and preferred them to stay put. Cody then visited both Carl Schurz, the secretary of the interior, and E. A. Hyat, commissioner of Indian Affairs, to point out that the employment he was offering could benefit both the Indians and the republic. Cody was required to post a bond for the use of the Indians. Sometimes $10,000 got him one hundred Indians, but sometimes the same amount only got him thirty. Cody's personal diplomacy worked—for many years he hired Indians—but the U.S. government was never entirely happy with the situation. Where Indians were concerned, the U.S. government wanted full control, a fact Cody realized to his sorrow many years later at the time of Sitting Bull's death. Probably Sherman's only-good-Indian-is-a-dead-Indian policy was still the dominant view.

3

THOSE who knew Buffalo Bill Cody well must have been a little shocked, if they were privy to the announcement of this first farewell tour, to discover that he intended to live out his days as a rancher and a gentleman farmer. Up to this point in time Cody had never exhibited the slightest interest in farming, gentlemanly or otherwise—and, if possible, had showed even less interest in ranching. His few statements about cowboy life in the autobiography are less than glowing, although by the time the book came out (1879) Cody *was* a rancher, if not a very enthusiastic one.

In fact, he went into the cattle business with Major Frank North, whose brother Luther so long and vehemently disputed Cody's never-too-insistent claim to have killed Tall Bull.

In 1877 neither Bill Cody nor Frank North owned a ranch, at least not in the accepted sense of the word. The large concerns, mostly British or Scottish, which began to acquire ranches in Wyoming and Montana operated on a very vast scale—though seldom profitably. Most of these enterprises were syndicates—they lost money steadily until they gave up; like plenty of high plains ranchers, many were ruined by the terrible winter of 1885–1886.

The notion that Cody would be a "gentleman farmer" will appear, to anyone who has spent time in North Platte, Nebraska, to be about as ludicrous as some of Ned Buntline's temperance speeches. In 1877 much of Nebraska was open range, owned merely by the U.S. government. Land agents had begun to appear—the writer Mari

114

Sandoz's famous father, Old Jules, was one of them—but naturally, the land agents were trying to sell the most appealing land, perhaps land watered by a spring or creek. Certainly at this time no one was trying to sell the Nebraska sand hills, or much rather bleak land north of the North Platte. Only a cracked land agent would have tried to sell the sand hills first.

In 1877 Cody and North went to Ogallala and purchased about fifteen hundred head of cattle, which they duly branded and drove north, to a promisingly grassy piece of acreage on the South Fork of the Dismal River. I have often thought that the Dismal River must be one of the most aptly named streams in our land; by horse it was about a day's ride north of North Platte—by car it can be reached from that city in about an hour.

Cody may, for a while, have attempted to convince himself that he liked cowboying, but in fact he and Frank North had hardly got the herd settled in up along the South Fork when Cody took himself off to the Red Cloud agency to recruit more show Indians for his next tour.

Why *would* he have liked ranch life in northern Nebraska, where there was a scarcity of female company and even saloons were few and far between? Also, it was already fairly obvious that the great American open range was about to become a thing of the past. The government might allow each family 160 acres, but 160 acres along the Dismal River would hardly support fifteen hundred head of cattle, much less the ten thousand that Cody had bragged about. Fortunately Cody and North managed to cash out just in time, selling the operation in 1882 for something like $75,000.

Bill Cody, the showman, was not entirely wasting his time with all those bovines. He noticed that cowboys were always competing with one another in roping contests or bronco-riding contests. Cody quickly concluded that if these ranch competitions could be organized, people might pay to see them. If such competitions could be linked to some patriotic theme or occasion, then *lots* of people might pay to see them. His own dislike of cowboying did not keep him from appreciating the skill of these young riders and ropers.

Probably Cody's central insight as an impresario was that it was always a good idea to link patriotism to performance. The Wild West, as it evolved under his leadership, was always, however crudely, a pageant of American life—and particularly that part of it that had involved the settling of the American West.

Cody's notion—even as he and Frank North were selling their cattle business—was to organize and promote a big cowboy competition in North Platte to celebrate the Fourth of July.

Where Wild West shows were concerned, Cody eventually had the best that were ever staged, but it's not clear that he had the first. Many troupes had, for some time, been wandering around America, most of them half circus and half Wild West show. Cody perfected the show and made it internationally viable as a form of entertainment, but several people were fumbling with the idea of converting the Wild West into entertainment.

Rodeo is a different matter. There had been informal ranch contests as long as there had been ranches, but few of these attracted more than local attention. Cody at once organized a rodeo that set the standard for what would become a very popular sport.

His rodeo was called the Old Glory Blow Out and was held in North Platte on the Fourth of July 1882. Cody had hoped to get as many as one hundred entrants in the contests; but as the time approached, he soon found that he had closer to one thousand. So popular was this first event that for a few days the great central plains became virtually depopulated: everybody seemed to be rushing to North Platte.

One reason this first rodeo was held in North Platte was because the city boasted a racetrack with a sturdy fence around it. Had Cody lacked a fenced arena, a good many spectators could easily have been trampled.

Rodeo caught on quickly. The very next year the town of Pecos, Texas, had a Fourth of July rodeo—Prescott, Arizona, and many other communities soon followed suit. Nowadays there is hardly a town in the West, large or small, that doesn't attempt to stage an annual rodeo. As a boy of nine I rode in the first rodeo in my hometown of Archer City, Texas—the community's sixtieth rodeo has just taken place, and all this because Buffalo Bill Cody, long ago in Nebraska, recognized that cowboys and the skills they practiced were an interesting part of the American experience. Ever since, rodeo has brought a bit of color to small-town life.

It was far from being one of Bill Cody's worst ideas.

4

I'VE said earlier that Buffalo Bill, in his mellow moods, while not exactly making light of his own achievements, didn't normally exaggerate them either—not unless he was lending himself to a promotion. He was as relaxed about his not very impressive career as an actor as he had been about those various skirmishes with Indians that, in his view, just didn't amount to much. He knew that the prairie-and-campfire melodramas he starred in with Texas Jack Omohundro and his wife, the "peerless Morlacchi," didn't amount to much, where theater was concerned.

But his Wild West shows, once hammered into workable form, *did* amount to something—they were the source of Cody's extraordinary celebrity, which, in his day, was not exceeded by anyone in the world. Celebrity did amount to much—Cody was one of the first performers to truly acquire superstardom.

Even in the innocence of the late nineteenth century celebrity seldom happened unless some effort was made. Queen Victoria was a celebrity because she was a queen; her fellow monarch Franz Josef was a celebrity not so much because he ruled an empire but because he had married—not happily—the most beautiful woman in Europe, the empress Elizabeth.

But Cody was not a royal; his origins were humble. He was an extraordinary horseman and, from his youth, a very handsome man. Looks and horsemanship combined to give him his start. Early on, as we have seen, even when he was doing fairly mundane work as a scout or hunter, he had a sense of image. When he had his first promotional photograph made, Matthew Brady took it—and was to take many, many more. In this first promotional photograph Cody is in scout's buckskins and is leaning on a rifle, probably his buffalo gun Lucretia Borgia. Joy Kasson's fine book shows how careful Cody was about his own iconography—he realized at once that his fortune depended on his looking the part of a Western frontiersman. He and his colleagues then evolved a complex outdoor operation in which national memory and popular history combined to form a visually and emotionally satisfying panorama. Photographs, posters, and book illustrations all had their job to do—before Cody was done, in 1917, many thousands of images of him had been seen by audiences in America and Western Europe. They are still being seen at Euro Disney.

The first of Buffalo Bill's Wild West shows from which at least some continuity can be traced was held in Omaha in 1883; the last, as I have mentioned, was in Chicago in 1916, which means that for about thirty years the onetime scout William F. Cody was engaged in putting on shows: indoor shows when a sports palace was available, outdoor shows when necessary. Many performers had their hour and departed. Annie Oakley performed with Cody for sixteen seasons but afterward exercised her talents in other forums.

In this thirty years of organizing large groups of people into workable teams and troupes, many managers, part managers, owners, half owners, banks, lawyers, accountants, and press agents devoted much energy to making sense of Bill Cody's tangled affairs. Most failed. His assets were threatened with seizure more than once, but since buffalo and Indians were among the assets, seizing them usually turned out to be more trouble than it was worth. Cody and Doc Carver once flipped a coin to determine who got what when they ended their brief, contentious partnership. Cody got the Deadwood stage.

It is not my intention in this book to chart the comings and goings of the many financial players involved. Sarah Blackstone has published two fine books on the business life of Buffalo Bill Cody. Her *Buckskins, Bullets, and Business* cannot be bettered as a study of the purely financial history of the Wild West shows.

Nor do I intend to plod through Cody's thirty-two seasons as a showman, describing the splendors and miseries of each.

What might be useful, though, is an annotated listing of the major characters who were involved with Cody and the shows. Many were once famous, and Cody and Annie Oakley are still famous; but most of these gifted or not so gifted folks are now just forgotten players from a bygone era. Giuseppina Morlacchi was a very beautiful woman who perhaps did bring the cancan to America, but the only book about herself and her husband, Texas Jack Omohundro, was published fifty years ago. One will find little trace of her today. The same can be said for Doc Carver, Pawnee Bill, and many others.

Buffalo Bill did manage to get his shows off the ground at the right time, just when outdoor spectacles became popular. The Ringling Brothers started their circus only a year later—at one time the Ringlings were part owners of Cody's show.

It should be emphasized that Cody did not advertise his spectacle as a "show." It was Buffalo Bill's Wild West, which meant that in his mind it was history—our history—and not just a collection of sharpshooters, trick riders, and the like. It was not, in his mind, a circus, although it contained many elements taken from the circus. What Cody wanted were tropes such as the attack on the Deadwood stage, or a battle between settlers and Indians, or himself taking the first scalp for Custer.

Cody's vision prevailed and is prevailing still, somewhere or other. When my county attained its centennial year, in 1980, the pageant put on every night for two weeks in our small rodeo arena was pure Cody.

All serious commentators on Cody's career agree on one thing: his shows succeeded—as, for example, did the TV miniseries of my own novel *Lonesome Dove* (125 million viewers)—because of the immense, worldwide appetite for anything pretending to portray life in the old West. In our time a Frenchman named George Fronval has published at least six hundred Western novelettes, and even in distant Norway there's a writer, named Kjell Halbing, who has produced more than sixty.

The thing to remember about this appetite for Westerns and the West is that the millions who possess it are *entirely* uncritical. They'll take anything in buckskins, literally. The Karl May cult in Germany has not even begun to slow down, although May died in 1912 and was himself never west of Buffalo. Indeed, as I discovered with *Lonesome Dove*, it is really impossible to get people to look at the West critically—they just refuse. The director John Ford is said to have decreed that if you have to choose between the truth and the legend, print the legend. From my experience I'd say that there's really no choice: for most readers and viewers it's the legend or nothing.

It seems that Bill Cody figured this out instinctively at the very beginning of his career. The Old Glory Blow Out in North Platte, plus the success of his various melodramas, which he knew to be terrible, combined to give him the necessary clue.

So, banking on his good looks and his horsemanship, he made it happen.

In the next few chapters I'll look at some of the people who either helped him make it happen or else got in his way.

5

ONE aspect of late-nineteenth-century performance that has long since gone the way of the passenger pigeon was the endurance shoot, in which contestants fired thousands of bullets or pellets at a variety of targets, including live pigeons. Some blame these shoots for the extinction of the passenger pigeons; the popularity of squab at high-end restaurants was another factor in the passenger pigeon's fade, along with habitat destruction, mass hunts, and the like. (The term "stool pigeon" derives from these stupendous all-day shoots. The stool pigeon was a decoy bird tethered to a stool or fence post.)

By the time of Buffalo Bill's Wild West the endurance shooters mainly shot at glass balls, trap-thrown, or wooden blocks. Captain Adam Bogardus, who shot with Cody's show on some occasions, had a hand in the invention of the skeet trap; he also may have been the first marathon shooter to use the Ligowsky clay pigeons, an invention which in time regularized skeet shooting, a sport that once enjoyed a much greater popularity than it does today. Annie Oakley and her husband, Frank Butler, ran a high-end skeet club after they had left Cody's show.

These endurance shoots were popular everywhere. Doc Carver did particularly well in the Hoboken area, where there were many German shooting clubs. It was not a sport for those with little stamina. In Brooklyn on one occasion Doc Carver broke 5,500 glass balls out of 6,211 thrown. Doc Carver and his opponents, of course, had loaders. Annie Oakley, on one occasion and perhaps one occasion only, shot 5,000 clay pigeons in a day, loading her own guns. She broke 4,772 or thereabouts.

The real problem in these endurance shoots, as Doc Carver testified, was eyestrain, the result of so much squinting. After the 6,000-ball shoot in Brooklyn, Carver had to go to bed with a cloth over his eyes for two days. Although he did more than anyone else to popularize these shoots, he was not, as he often claimed, the absolute top marathon shooter of his day—the title probably belonged to one Adolph Topperwein, who committed only nine misses out of 72,500 balls thrown.

On the other hand, Doc Carver made his living as a competitive shooter for almost half a century, taking on all comers in advertised shoots in America, Europe, and Australia. He probably shot more shots, most of which hit their targets, than any competitive shooter of his day.

W. F. Carver and W. F. Cody had been rivals to some degree since their buffalo-hunting days. They ran into one another in New Haven in 1883 and immediately decided to put on a Wild West show together. Carver claimed that he already had a Wild West show and merely invited Cody to come in as an act of generosity. The reader should be warned that absolutely everything that Cody and Carver said about one another, in the course of a rivalry that lasted at least four decades, should be taken with a large grain of salt. When speaking of one another, neither is to be believed.

What is true is that the first show operated by Cody and Carver was the same show that opened in Omaha in May of 1883. It boasted a title that many would consider cumbersome: "The Wild West, W. F. Cody and W. F. Carver's Rocky Mountain and Prairie Exhibition." Carver wanted to get in the phrase "Golden West," a locution he was fond of and later used in his independent productions.

Like many first efforts the show did not go off seamlessly. A number of Omaha dignitaries, including the mayor, were invited to ride in the Deadwood stage while it came under mock attack from a party of Pawnees. The Pawnees had been recruited by Frank North. As soon as the Indians started whooping and hollering, the mules panicked and made several bouncy circuits of the arena before they could be stopped. This indignity so angered the mayor of Omaha that he had to be restrained from attacking Cody physically.

Doc Carver was six years older than Bill Cody, but outlived him by a decade, perhaps because he didn't drink as heavily—which is not to imply that he was actually reluctant to bend the elbow. He was born in Illinois and, like Cody, was on his own at an early age. He was a teamster for a time, did some scouting, fought in several skirmishes with Indians, and like Cody, was a professional buffalo hunter. He was probably a better overall marksman than Cody; when shooting competitions began to be popular he soon figured out that shooting at glass balls or tossed coins was a lot easier than the demanding life of the frontier.

Carver was not as good-looking as Cody, nor was he as immediately acceptable to rich people—though, in time, he acquired polish and was not far behind Cody when it came to seducing, socially, the rich and the royal. He was practically the only one of Cody's close rivals who developed a real animus against him, the basis for which may have been mostly financial. From the time of that first show in Omaha the two could never agree about how much one partner owed the other. Carver claimed that Cody originally agreed to put in $27,000 but instead stayed drunk most of the summer and never put in a cent. Cody's bankers, though not denying that Cody had a tendency to go on what he called "toots," claimed that the financial situation was the other way around. They insisted that Carver didn't put in a cent, either—yet somehow the show got mounted, and expensively, too. For the next several years the two showmen made various legal lunges at one another, most of them inconclusive. Cody may have offered to flip a coin to settle the matter, but Carver was not charmed by the gamble. Coins were flipped, perhaps, and Cody did surrender $10,000 at one point, while keeping possession of the Deadwood stage.

Doc Carver billed himself as the "Spirit Gun of the West," whatever that means, but many who worked with him called him the "Evil Spirit of the West." Though never quite as famous as Cody, he was famous enough and industrious enough to eventually get bookings on three continents. His temper, to say the least, was uncertain. Once, at Coney Island, he broke his rifle over his horse's head; similar flare-ups were frequent. Still, most of his performers seemed to like him, and tolerate his outbursts, but the idealized fame that Cody won eluded the Spirit Gun—even though he won hundreds of shooting competitions. Cody won none.

Among Carver's partners was Cody's friend the poet-scout Jack Crawford (the father, perhaps, of cowboy poetry). Carver was awarded almost as many medals and prizes as Cody—he ended up with a wagonload of fancy guns. He bragged about these trophies but they didn't soothe his restless spirit much. He married and acquired a ranch in California but that didn't soothe his restless spirit either. Within weeks he would be back to mounting shows. When Cody took his troupe to Europe in 1887 Carver was not far behind. Occasionally, to the annoyance of both, they would show up in the same European city at the same time. This happened in Hamburg in 1890. Since the two troupes hated, or professed to hate, one another, the citizenry of that stout German city were, for a time, terrified, at least in the opinion of a reporter for the *New York World:* "Hamburg is filled with a howling mob of Indians and cowboys who are awaiting the chance to scalp one another. As soon as Cody's bills are posted, Carver's assistants come along and tear them down."

It may be that, in the long run, Carver did better in Europe than Cody because he traveled with a smaller, more manageable troupe. Cody took ninety-seven Indians and lots of white performers, not to mention an extensive crew, when he first went to England, in 1887. Carver got by with twenty Indians and a few other acts. His ace in the hole was his own shooting. It always seemed to please crowds, though not as much as Annie Oakley's shooting pleased crowds.

Carver took his troupe to places such as St. Petersburg and Australia, where Cody had never worked up to going. Russia was not easy to get into but Carver applied to Ulysses S. Grant himself; Grant got the players in under a kind of blanket visa.

Despite his fits and frequent surliness, Carver was a man of considerable principle. When he reached Australia he was appalled to discover that beautiful parrots and ibises were being destroyed in planned shoots; he loudly spoke against the practice. In San Francisco he attacked the local merchants for their too frequent use of wooden Indians, which he considered an insult to the real Indians, members of a noble race, that he himself had just brought around the world.

Doc Carver survived and kept shooting. He outlived another sharpshooter, Annie Oakley, by a year. He remained to the end his own man, although to continue to compete in the cutthroat world of road shows he had to constantly scramble to develop new acts.

Toward the end Doc Carver's acts became more like boardwalk attractions. He invested in some diving horses and even a diving elk. A female daredevil rode the horses off a forty-foot platform into a fourteen-foot tank, which certainly took guts on the part of the daredevils.

The elk, so far as I can discover, dove alone.

6

JOHN Y. NELSON, whose Sioux name was Cha Sha Sha Opogeo, was one of the few plainsmen to stay on good terms with Wild Bill Hickok, Doc Carver, and Buffalo Bill Cody (a moody triumvirate), though John Y. Nelson himself was a man of uncertain temperament. He sometimes sustained deadly feuds for decades. His status among the Sioux was especially high because he was married to Red Cloud's daughter, who eventually bore him a vast brood, which he insisted on traveling with despite various impresarios' reluctance. His most conspicuous physical attribute was a magnificent full beard. Perhaps it was the beard that attracted photographers—John Y. Nelson appears in many photos.

Nelson worked for both Carver and Cody but the appearance that contributed most to his fame occurred in London. On the night that four kings rode in the Deadwood stage, John Y. Nelson, with his bushy beard and his inscrutable manner, rode shotgun. There is a famous photograph of the four not unapprehensive kings sitting in the stagecoach and of John Y. Nelson, equipped with shotgun, inscrutably observing it all. The kings were of Austria, Denmark, Saxony, and Greece. What John Y. Nelson may have been inscrutably considering was whether the Deadwood stage—a vehicle that had careened around too many arenas, chased by too many Indians, for too long—would fall apart, with all those nobs inside it. The kings themselves did not impress him.

The show's manager, Nate Salsbury, who firmly held the line on expenses, had failed either to purchase a new stagecoach or to have the existing one repaired.

But Cody, taking no chances, drove the stage himself. Judging from other photographs, Cody seems pretty tense. Perhaps he was remembering the runaway in Omaha, and his near fistfight with the outraged mayor. Still, having four kings in the stagecoach plus the Prince of Wales, who sat on the driver's seat with Cody and John Y. Nelson, was thumping good publicity. Major Burke, the press agent, was of course ecstatic.

John Y. Nelson stayed with Cody through many tours and many vicissitudes. In group pictures of the troupe he is usually seen in the front row, seated with his wife and many lively children. Without his beard he would have closely resembled the Italian peasant whose shack is nearly shaken to pieces by the close passage of trains, in Sergio Leone's *For a Few Dollars More*.

7

WHEN Cody and Carver and their soon-to-be rival Gordon Lillie (Pawnee Bill) began to drift into the performing life at the beginning of the 1880s, it was in part because, behind them to the west, the frontier as they had known it was closing. They were vigorous men with an abundance of frontier skills which were rapidly becoming obsolete. Railroads girdled the continent; and the telegraph, the singing wires, carried messages a lot quicker than anything Russell, Majors, and Waddell could have devised. In distant Arizona the Apache wars continued but otherwise the native warriors of the plains and forests were no longer a threat.

Cody, Carver, and Lillie all had wives, but none of them could be described as well domesticated. They were vagabonds and soldiers of fortune. What did they do now? What would their model be?

When Bill Cody set out on his "farewell tour" to California he described himself as a theatrical star—perhaps it was Major Burke who supplied the term. At this point in time what we now call the star system—mainly just a method of financing shows of one kind or another—was not well advanced. But in Cody's case the description was not unfair. If any retired scout and part-time actor could be called a star, it was he. Thanks to the dime novels and more or less constant press coverage he was much better known than any of the other frontierless frontiersmen.

The one true superstar in the theatrical world in this time was Sarah Bernhardt (Henriette-Rosine Bernard), who, from her base at the Théâtre Français, made frequent appearances both in England

and in New York. Even losing a leg didn't stop the Divine Sarah—she continued to work and outlived Cody by six years.

When, in 1883, Nate Salsbury signed a partnership contract with Bill Cody and the then-reigning sharpshooter, Captain Adam Bogardus, to form an entity called "Buffalo Bill's Wild West—America's National Entertainment," it is doubtful that he expected Cody's fame to so completely eclipse his own (and Bogardus's too, of course). In the theatrical world of that time there was a fair sprinkling of stars, one of whom was Nate Salsbury himself. General William Tecumseh Sherman remembered the young Nate Salsbury, aged perhaps sixteen, delivering an uplifting version of "Oh! Susanna," at an impromptu entertainment during the difficult Georgia campaign. Nate survived a period at the dreadful Andersonville prison and briefly pursued the study of law before devoting himself permanently to the theater.

Nate Salsbury was not ungifted, either as actor or playwright. He rose to be leading man at a theater in Chicago, but soon left to form his own troupe, which he called the Troubadours, a troupe he kept together for about a dozen years. Like Doc Carver he even took his actors to Australia. His specialty was light farces, one of which, *Patchwork*, achieved an eighteen-month run. Another, called *The Brook*, played successfully for about five years.

Thus, when he made his contract with Cody, it was star joining star; and as a longtime man of the theater, Salsbury's skills were much sharper and his experience much broader than Cody's. Also, when necessary, he could write. Cody, despite the flamboyance of his autobiography, really couldn't.

In our day we have many superstars to choose from, but in Cody's day they were thin on the ground and at first no one—certainly not Nate Salsbury—was willing to consider Cody a superstar. He was not the Divine Sarah.

Major Burke, whom Salsbury regarded as a necessary evil—somebody had to hustle up publicity in order to get out the crowds—might call Cody a star but to Salsbury, at first, the man remained a tall, frequently drunk, former scout. Gordon Lillie, who became the manager of the show at one point, did like Major Burke, or at least approved of the job he did.

The more complicated question is whether Salsbury really *liked*

Cody, or whether one star's envy of another star's immense success colored their relationship almost from the first. It quickly became apparent to Salsbury and everyone else that the tall former scout was going to be a very big star indeed.

Nate Salsbury wrote a memoir, but in his lifetime made no attempt to publish it. Some of it saw magazine publication many years after all the principals were dead. It was a jaundiced memoir, though rarely really mean. Salsbury may have been the first to see that Cody was becoming dependent on the adulation of the very people who were bleeding him financially; he also made a real effort to get control of Cody's drinking, which was heavy. When Salsbury finally got Cody to agree to limit his intake to one drink a day Cody foiled him by securing a tankard that held at least a quart of whiskey. Cody, from his jayhawking days on, made no secret of his fondness for drink. Once, in apologizing to the poet-scout Jack Crawford for being so slow to answer an inquiry, he excused himself thusly: "I was on a hell of a toot and I seldom attend to anything except hoof her up when I am that way."

Others dispute the stories of Cody's excessive drinking. It was obvious that he enjoyed his liquor but he usually managed to show up sober when the occasion was serious enough to demand it.

Nate Salsbury possessed excellent managerial skills, and he, of course, had a stake in the success of the Wild West too. At first he applied his skills to the task of keeping the company solvent, until Cody's extraordinary charisma kicked in, first nationwide and, eventually, worldwide.

The reader will remember that it was Salsbury who, in only a few minutes that day in Louisville, recognized Annie Oakley's star quality and ordered all those posters. He was thus midwife to the birth of our first huge superstars, Buffalo Bill and Annie Oakley. Salsbury was probably as surprised as anybody at how broad their celebrity became.

Nate Salsbury probably had enough of a performer's ego to be a little sour when Cody put him so wholly in the shade; he couldn't resist sniping at Cody a bit, but whatever jealousy he felt did not destroy his judgment or his showmanship. Though his name appeared as proprietor on all programs, he was not required to merge his troupe with Cody's or to be with the Wild West for every performance. In fact he was performing in Denver when the first of many calamities overtook the Wild West. The troupe was on a steamboat headed down the Mississippi to New Orleans when the boat hit another steamer and sank. The crew, the troupe, and most of the horses survived, but the elk and the buffalo, Captain Bogardus's guns, and many props went to the bottom. Salsbury was about to step onto a stage in Denver when he received a succinct telegram from Cody: "Outfit at bottom of river, what do you advise?"

According to Don Russell the coolheaded Nate Salsbury merely asked the conductor to repeat the overture while he scribbled a telegram to Cody saying, "Go to New Orleans, reorganize, and open on your date."

Cody did manage to reorganize and to open on his date, but otherwise, their run at the New Orleans Exposition was one of the low points of Cody's career. It rained for forty-four days, during which the Wild West doggedly performed, but to very poor turnouts. The shipwreck, the rain, and other difficulties left the Wild West $60,000 in the red; there were other difficulties too. Frank North, Cody's old friend, was seriously injured when a girth broke; he died in the spring, by which time it is unlikely either North or Cody really knew or really cared which of them killed Tall Bull.

The Sells Circus was in New Orleans at the same time as the Wild West—occasionally the bored performers would visit back and forth, one of them a small woman from Ohio who called herself Annie Oakley. Not long afterward, she had her famous audition in Louisville.

Cody left New Orleans vowing to go on a drunk that would really be a drunk. Probably he kept this vow, but when and where and with whom is not recorded.

8

WE are not through with Nate Salsbury and the management of the Wild West, a long involvement with a few breaks in it. Like some presidents, Cody was a man of overflowing, at times overpowering, energies. He quickly wore people down, his wife, Louisa, among them. Much as she complained about her Billy's absences, when he did show up he was likely to have a mob with him, a mob that would likely have taxed the patience of any wife.

Salsbury too probably had periods of Cody fatigue. Sometimes he needed a breather, and went his own way for a while. Still, he had a clear mandate to manage everything: salaries, personnel, transport. It was he who set the order in which performers appeared. But when Cody was around it became impossible to maintain a clear separation of powers. Cody regarded it as *his* show; he could not resist meddling in everything: particularly personnel. To the end of his days, almost, he insisted on employing numerous former scouts or old army men whom he had known in frontier times: Frank North, Bob Haslam, John Y. Nelson were among this group but there were many others. Cody's incessant meddling no doubt irritated Salsbury and led to his occasional disappearances—though he took care never to be out of reach of the telegraph. Nowadays he would have bristled with cell phones. His instant response to the sinking of the steamboat is indicative of his capacity to maintain some measure of oversight.

Even though the first two seasons lost money it was clear that the show would draw plenty of customers once certain operational problems had been dealt with. By the third season, 1885, Buffalo Bill's Wild West made a profit. This was the year that Annie Oakley joined the troupe.

Another benefit Salsbury derived from his little absences was that he would not have to be irked by the fulsome behavior of the press agent, Major Burke. Veterans with long memories recalled that Burke himself had once been a performer who called himself Arizona John. One reason Salsbury came to dislike Burke was because the press agent absolutely worshiped Cody. He was puppylike in his need for Cody's approval, which, mostly, he had. With the troupe in America Burke mostly stayed on top of his tasks, which mainly involved tooting Cody's horn to a lot of editors, journalists, and advertising men.

Once the troupe began to travel about Europe, however, opportunities for mismanagement were sharply increased. Sometimes Burke lost his interpreter, the result being that the Wild West ship might dock, or train arrive, with no one there to help them unload.

One such arrival occurred in Naples. Burke was nowhere to be seen, there was no one there to help load, and the bemused Italians merely gaped at them. When Burke did show up, drenched in sweat and very anxious, Cody promptly fired him, and fired him in the thunderous tones he summoned when he lost his temper.

Salsbury was enjoying a vacation in London when this telegram reached him, its author being Major Burke: "My scalp hangs in the tepee of Pahaska at the foot of Mount Vesuvius. Please send me money to take me back to the Land of the Free and the Home of the Brave."

Before Salsbury could even figure out what the ruckus was about, Cody's fit passed, and as Louisa Cody says in her book, "the god and his admirer were arm in arm once more."

The god and his admirer? Louisa was not exaggerating when she labels Burke's feeling for Cody as being little short of idolatry; her book, *Memories of Buffalo Bill*, contains the most generous appraisal we have of the gregarious Major Burke.

Lulu Cody's book is an odd but not unreadable production. She mentions very few of the troupers: mainly just Cody, Burke, and the young sharpshooter Johnny Baker. Nate Salsbury—she spells it "Salisbury"—comes in for a few cautious mentions. Probably Lulu suspected that Salsbury didn't worship Cody—a sin in her book—although she herself was far from worshipful where Bill Cody was concerned.

Virtually the only woman mentioned in *Memories of Buffalo Bill* was Mlle. Morlacchi, the premiere danseuse and wife of Texas Jack Omohundro. The reason Mlle. Morlacchi came in for so much mention was that Major Burke had a mad but hopeless crush on her. Lulu Cody happens to have been the person Major Burke chose to confide in, while in the grip of this hopeless passion. The position of confidante appealed to Lulu, as it does to most women; she and Major Burke spent a good deal of time together, talking about nothing else. In fact the premiere danseuse and the tall scout were happily married, leaving Major Burke to nurse his longing in vain.

An odd aspect of Lulu Cody's memoir is that it is a free-flowing time line, with very few dates given. Now we're in Leavenworth, or Hays City, or Rochester, or North Platte; it's hard to say on a given page whether the Codys had been married two years or twenty. Lulu definitely remembers opening the box and finding Yellow Hair's smelly scalp in it. When Bill comes home and regales the girls with a colorful account of his famous "duel," which, in this telling, was a knife fight pure and simple, Lulu displays no doubt.

In *Memories of Buffalo Bill* Lulu Cody comes across as a spunky woman who is going to have her say, and precisely her say. She blandly leaves out all discord, admits only once or twice to loneliness, and generally paints as admiring a picture of her husband as even Major Burke could have produced. No mention of other women sullies her pages; even Little Missie is not allowed to appear. Then, with no warning, we're at the end:

> Many a year followed that, many a year of wandering, while Will went from country to country, from nation to nation, from state to state. There were fat times and there were lean times, there were times when storms gathered, and there were times when the sun shone; but always in cloud or sunshine, there was ever a shadow just behind

him [Cody], following him with a wistful love that few men can ever display, Major John M. Burke. And when the time came for that Will and I said goodbye forever, another man loosed his hold on the world. Throughout every newspaper office in the country, where John Burke had sat by the hour, never mentioning a word about himself, but telling always of the progress of his "god" there flashed the news that Major John M. Burke, the former representative of William Frederick Cody, had become dangerously ill. And six weeks later the faithful old hands were folded, the lips that had spoken hardly anything but praise of Buffalo Bill for half a century, were still. Major Burke had died when Cody died, only his body lingered on for those six weeks, at last to loose its hold on the loving, faithful old spirit it bound and allow it to follow its master over the Great Divide.

The death of Cody himself is recorded less grandiloquently; then, a few pages on, it's Lulu's turn.

Yes, my life is lived, and out here in the West, where every evening brings a more wonderful, more beautiful blending at sunset, I watch the glorious colorings and feel a sense of satisfaction that it will not be long now before I see the fading of the sunset of my own little world, until the time shall come when I am with the children I loved and the man I loved . . . on the Trail Beyond.

Lulu had indeed outlived her children and Bill Cody. She outlived Texas Jack Omohundro by forty years, and his lovely wife, the peerless Morlacchi, by thirty-four. Texas Jack Omohundro died of pneumonia in Leadville, Colorado, in 1880, and his wife, the premiere danseuse so admired by Major Burke, succumbed to cancer in Lowell, Massachusetts, in 1886. Nate Salsbury went in 1902, Cody in 1917, Lulu in 1920. But three of the best rifle shots ever, Johnny Baker, Doc Carver, and Annie Oakley, were still going strong.

9

ONE thing we've learned in the celebrity-rich last century is superstars cleave to other superstars. Rock stars hang out with other rock stars, movie stars with other movie stars, Michael Jordan with Larry Bird, and so on.

By 1886, when Cody and Salsbury brought the Wild West to the Erastina resort on Staten Island for an extended stay, Cody had become such a huge star that he had no peer to hang out with. Fortunately he had an entourage, and Annie Oakley's star was rising rapidly. At some time during this season Sitting Bull went home, but not before Cody presented him with a gray horse and a fine sombrero; in later years the difficult Hunkpapa was very particular about this hat. When one of his relatives decided to try it on, Sitting Bull was not pleased: "My friend Long Hair gave me this hat. I value it very highly, for the hand that placed it on my head had a friendly feeling for me."

Before departing Sitting Bull made his "Little Sure Shot," Annie Oakley, a member of the Hunkpapa tribe.*

After the sinking of the steamboat and the huge losses they incurred in their first two seasons, Cody and Salsbury had to give seri-

---

* Sitting Bull had first seen Annie shoot in a theater in St. Paul in 1884. He sent $65 to her room in hopes of getting a photograph. She sent the money back but went to see him the next day. Adoption into the tribe, she later noted, would have secured her "five ponies, a wigwam, and no end of cattle."

ous consideration to profits, which could best be achieved, it seemed to them, by settling in for an extended run in a big population center such as New York. This might produce not only famous spectators but also repeat spectators. Staten Island, where P. T. Barnum had first chased his buffalo, proved to be nearly ideal.

Soon enough celebrities began to attend the Wild West, and they were not sparing of endorsements. General Sherman attended the first show and uttered some fairly cryptic praise. P. T. Barnum himself was more direct. "They do not need spangles to make it a real show," he said. Libbie Custer proclaimed the Wild West "the most realistic and faithful representation of a western life that has ceased to be, with advancing civilization."

Mark Twain was even more fulsome, claiming that the Wild West

> brought back to me the breezy, wild life of the Rocky Mountains and stirred me like a war song. Down to its smallest detail the show is genuine—cowboys, vaqueros, Indians, stagecoach, costumes and all; it is wholly free from sham and insincerity and the effect produced on me by its spectacles were identical with those wrought upon me a long time ago by the same spectacles on the frontier . . . it is often said on the other side of the water that none of the exhibitions which we send to England are purely and distinctively American. If you will take the Wild West show over there you can remove that reproach.

Twain's enthusiasm for the Wild West never waned; he even went so far as to write a short story from the point of view of Cody's horse.

Long before the troupe did depart for England, in 1887, Cody had collected a bale of highly complimentary letters from virtually every prominent American military leader: Sherman, Sheridan, Crook, Merritt, and Bankhead, just to name the generals who wrote glowingly about Cody's splendid behavior. At least a score of colonels also weighed in.

The odd thing about these testimonials is that they all praise the show's realism, opinions contradicted—to my mind at least—by the many thousands of photographs of these same performances. What was realistic about Annie Oakley shooting glass balls? The only thing Western about her act was her costumes—she wore boots, which few Western women did at the time. The *events* that were most realistic, such as King of the Cowboys Buck Taylor's bronc riding, were closer to rodeo than to Indian fights and buffalo chases. The same could be said of the roping act of the champion vaquero Antonio Esquivel.

Somehow Cody succeeded in taking a very few elements of Western life—Indians, buffalo, stagecoach, and his own superbly mounted self—and creating an illusion that successfully stood for a reality that had been almost wholly different. Even hardened journalists such as Brick Pomeroy took fairly crude stagecraft for realism:

It is not a show. It is a resurrection, or rather an importation of the honest features of wild Western life and pioneer incidents to the East, that men, women, and children may see, realize, understand, and forever remember what the Western pioneers met, encountered, and overcame. It is in secular life what Christ and the apostles proposed to be in religious life, except that in this case there are no counterfeits but actual, living, powerful, very much alive and in earnest delegates from the West, all of whom have most effectively participated in what they here reproduce as a most absorbing educational realism.

The *Montreal Gazette* was no less convinced of the show's fidelity to the life that had been:

The whole thing is real. There is not a bit of claptrap about it. It is the picture of frontier life painted in intense realism, each scene standing forth in bold relief—painted, did I say? No, not painted, but acted as it is being acted along the entire frontier line that stretches from the Gulf of Mexico to the Great Slave Lake. It is a place and a scene to visit, therefore, not for mere amusement, but for the sake of studying in a school where all lessons are objective and in which have been gathered materials for observation and instruction which, in the nature of things, are perishable and soon destined to vanish.

Both these reports to a large degree affirm to the success of Cody's instinctive decision not to call the show a *show*. It was, in his mind, and in the minds of most of the spectators, history, not fiction—easy to understand fiction that allowed the audience to participate vicariously in the great and glorious adventure that had been the settling of the West, an enterprise not yet wholly concluded even in 1886.

According to the now famous Professor Frederick Jackson Turner, the American frontier finally closed in 1893, seven years after Cody and Salsbury brought their troupe to Staten Island. A fair number of performers in the Wild West had been frontiersmen, many of them old friends of Cody; all of the Indians were, of course, Indians. And yet the claim that the skits were wonderfully realistic still startles—though, by the low standards of the day, perhaps they were: Cody, after all, had begun his career as an actor in Western melodramas so crudely staged that red flannel was used for scalps.

On the prop level, at least, Buffalo Bill's Wild West did considerably better than that, despite which wholly unrealistic elements frequently crept in. In the real West, contra Mark Twain, few marksmen felt confident enough to shoot *behind* themselves, with the help of a mirror, as Annie Oakley did. The Deadwood stage, which Cody won in a coin flip, was real enough, but Cody's obsession with warbonnets wasn't. The Indians in the show were much more gloriously feathered than they could have afforded to be back at the Red Cloud agency, or even in pre-Custer times. There is a famous photograph in Carolyn Thomas Foreman's book about Indians abroad in which a relaxed crowd is watching two Indians playing Ping-Pong, all the while trailing full-length warbonnets and wearing white buckskins.

Realistic or not, Buffalo Bill's Wild West drew enormous crowds during its long Staten Island run. On a single sunny week in July nearly two hundred thousand spectators took the ferry and saw the show. For the portion of the crowd that had never been west of the Hudson, the skits and playlets probably did seem like the real thing—after all, it was pretty close to what they had been told the West was like in all those dime novels Ned Buntline and Prentiss Ingraham had been providing them with.

Mark Twain's credulity seems a bit harder to fathom. He was more or less in the publishing business by then—perhaps he thought a little adroit flattery might encourage the wildly popular Cody to become one of his authors. Or he could have been drunk. We must hope he was drunk when he penned "A Horse's Tale," the short story written from the point of view of Cody's show horse.

The turnout for the Staten Island run was extremely cheering to Cody and Salsbury: a show that had fumbled through two seasons, losing both money and personnel, found its footing in 1885 and solidified it with the long Staten Island run. It finally looked like a viable proposition, one that could make the two principals a lot of money. Perhaps it was Twain's remark about the low quality of our theatrical exports that got the two men to thinking about England.

But before we shepherd our ever-expanding troupe aboard the good ship *State of Nebraska* it is time to consider in more depth the blossoming career of Little Missie, the small but formidable woman whom few ever managed to outshoot.

Annie

1

BUFFALO BILL CODY wore his heart on his sleeve—all his life he was a soft touch, a partygoer and party giver who was never reluctant to pick up the tab. His kindness to the old buffalo hunter William Mathewson, perhaps the first hunter to be called Buffalo Bill, has already been noted. If he came across a homeless or impoverished youth he would sometimes keep him with the troupe as an errand boy, as he himself had once been. Both Dan Muller, the artist, and Johnny Baker, the sharpshooter, attracted Cody's sympathies—both were allowed to earn their pay. Cody at least provided a roof over their heads, and a little schooling.

Annie Oakley was as tightfisted as Cody was openhanded. Among the troupers she was thought to be as tight as Hetty Green, the so-called Witch of Wall Street. Some thought that Annie subsisted entirely on the free lemonade that Cody and Salsbury made available to everyone in the troupe. Most of her fellow performers forgave her this and loved her anyway. It was mainly her rivals who used her frugality as a point of attack. At the height of her fame she softened a bit, sometimes serving tea and cookies to whatever youngsters wandered up. But tea and cookies were about the limit of her largesse.

Annie was not Cody—she never wore her heart on her sleeve. She was interviewed often but she rarely exposed much of herself. What she felt as she became one of the most famous women on earth we don't really know. She did have a heart, as well as a more or less normal allotment of performer's ego. She made no secret of her disdain for female rivals such as Lillian Smith. The women of the troupe were not a sisterhood; had there been an effort to form one, it is unlikely that Annie Oakley would have been much help.

She was married to Frank Butler for about four decades; he was one of the few people Annie seemed genuinely comfortable with, and yet it is possible to wonder if she allowed even her husband to know her real feelings. She always dressed modestly—she never performed in pants. She was only five feet tall and, for most of her life, weighed only a little more than one hundred pounds, and yet she had made a profound impact on crowds. She was attractive, but not a raving beauty. As a performer she was animated, skipping into the arena and launching rapidly into her various shooting acts. Once she had become famous her appearances rarely lasted more than ten minutes, a fact she reflected on when she was introduced to the old Austrian emperor Franz Josef in 1890:

> I really felt sorry when I looked into the face of the Emperor of Austria . . . his face looked both tired and troubled. I then and there decided that being just plain Annie Oakley, with ten minutes work once or twice a day, was good enough for me, for I had, or at least I thought I had, my freedom.

Franz Josef was to plug on for twenty-five more years, doing his lonely and vexatious job; Annie was wise to note that his was not a role to be envied. She was often dead on the mark when assessing European royalty.

Cody always called Annie "Missie" and she was usually described in promotional materials as a "little girl" from the West who just happened to be an unparalleled rifle and wing shot. Her purity was always part of the sell, but so was her attractiveness, her seductiveness, even. The one visible sign of sex was her long lustrous hair. Occasionally she allowed herself to be photographed with it hanging loose, which certainly made a womanly appeal.

Where the real Annie was in all of this is impossible to tell and was always impossible to tell. Her husband, Frank Butler, the man who knew her best, published a few sporting articles about guns or fishing but, except for one or two husbandly jibes about her hatred of housekeeping, Frank Butler kept mum.

The Butlers were childless, which doesn't mean that the marriage was sexless. Annie wanted no male hand to touch her once she was dead, but what she may have wanted in the way of touching while she was alive cannot now be determined. She did, however, dote on her dogs, and she also exhibited maternal concern for young Johnny Baker, once he joined the show; she also took an interest in his children when they came along.

There is much about Annie Oakley that we will never know—in her own lifetime very few would claim to know her well.

So far as her life as a performer went, the mystery was surely part of the potency.

2

THE roots of Oakley's frugality are not hard to account for: in her girlhood she had known great poverty. She was born in Darke County, Ohio, in 1860, though she unabashedly changed her birth date to 1866 when the fifteen-year-old sharpshooter Lillian Smith joined Cody's show.* To the end of her life she casually lied about her age, though her lopping off of the six years did not go entirely unnoticed in the papers. The change is one more indication of her steely will. What she didn't accept, she altered, and then ignored the alteration, pretending that it had always been thus.

In any case, Charles Dickens had nothing on Annie Oakley when it came to a bad childhood. Annie's parents, Susan and Jacob Moses (or Mozee), were very poor; the situation then became desperate when Jacob Moses froze to death while attempting to bring supplies home through a blizzard. Susan Moses was destitute. One of Annie's sisters was given away to a family who offered to raise her. Though Annie killed her first bird at six and her first squirrel at eight, she was as yet too small to support her family by hunting.

At ten Annie was sent to the county poor farm, a place called the Infirmary. She was soon more or less leased out to a farmer who

---

* There were normally three shooting acts per show: Annie's, Lillian Smith's, and Johnny Baker's. Captain Adam Bogardus had been Cody's first sharpshooter. His decision to go on his own prompted Annie's famous audition in Louisville. "She's a daisy!" Salsbury reportedly said. "She'll easily put Bogardus in the shade."

needed help with his milking. Annie never identified this farmer, or his wife—she referred to them merely as the "wolves," and it was with the "wolves" that she spent the darkest hours of her childhood. She was overworked, starved, and beaten; once the wife put her out in a storm to freeze, but the husband, who had no intention of losing his slave, arrived in time to save her. She continued to be overworked and physically abused until she turned twelve, at which point she ran away and walked back to the poor farm, a distance of some forty miles. By this time, fortunately, the Infirmary was run by a nice couple named the Edingtons, who soon put Annie in charge of their sizable dairy. They even paid her a wage, most of which Annie saved, as she was to do throughout her life. Nancy Edington taught her to embroider—needlework soon became a passion, one she was to pursue throughout all her touring years. It was what she did in her tent, when she wasn't practicing her act.

The Edingtons also put Annie in school, where she proved a quick learner. At about age fifteen she went back to her mother, who had remarried. Very soon Annie worked out a deal with the grocers Samson and Katzenberger, who had a flourishing grocery in Greenville, Ohio. They had known Annie from before and liked her. They soon agreed to buy whatever small game she cleaned and shipped to town. One thing the grocers noticed right away was that the quail, rabbit, or grouse Annie sent was not shot or torn up. She either caught the game in snares or shot them through the head, so the meat would be prime. The grocers liked her so much that they presented her with a new shotgun. She was then only in her midteens, but from that time on, one way or another, Annie Oakley made her living with her gun.

3

WHY human beings like what they like or, to put it more strongly, obsess over what they're obsessed with, remains—despite much psychological commentary—a mystery. There's just no accounting for taste, and no way to know why Annie Oakley liked guns so much and mastered them so easily.

But like them she did. *Her* creation myth, to be put beside Cody's first Indian, involved a squirrel that lingered on the family fence too long, until Annie managed to pull down her father's big muzzle-loading rifle, propped it on the windowsill, and shot the squirrel right through the head. She always claimed that it was one of the better shots she ever made.

There is a somewhat less romantic version of Annie Oakley's first shot—in this version her brother hands her a shotgun, hoping the kick will discourage her and stop her from pestering him about guns. The kick breaks her nose but of course she brings down the bird.

The old muzzle-loading gun was much too heavy for Annie, but she did her best, often depending on snares and traps of various kinds to help her secure rabbits and quail. From the first she seems to have had absolute confidence in her shooting; she kept this confidence all her life. Ted Williams and Joe DiMaggio were said to be the exceptional hitters that they were because their eyesight was so keen that they could see the seams of the baseball as it came toward them. Perhaps Annie Oakley too had better eyesight than most. She gave many shooting clinics once she left Cody's tour; she taught her students correct posture and the importance of an easy swing; her teachings made it all sound simple—indeed, almost Zenlike: "You must have your mind, your nerve, and everything in harmony. Don't look at your gun, simply follow the object with the end of it, as if the tip of your barrel was the point of your finger."

She herself never seemed so clearly in a state of harmony as when she was shooting her gun. Many opponents observed this. Somehow she remained supremely ladylike when firing a rifle or shotgun, weapons which had largely been the domain of the male until she came along. During her first English tour she had her worst day of shooting ever, trying to hit a swift variety of pigeons called blue rocks. The shoot was held at a gentlemen's shooting club. Annie, shooting a gun that was too heavy, with shot too light for the windy weather, only managed to hit five pigeons out of twenty, a deep embarrassment for her. But the gentleman who managed the club, who had not been impressed with Lillian Smith, *was* impressed with Annie. He told her that she was much less of a shot than he expected, but much more of a lady.

A fine English gunsmith named Charles Lancaster was there that day, and at once figured out what was wrong. He persuaded Annie to let him make her a lighter gun, a twelve-gauge that only weighed six pounds. Before she left England she tried the blue rocks several more times, eventually managing to bring down forty-one out of fifty.

But this is to get far ahead of the story. The shotgun the Greenville grocers gave Annie was a Parker sixteen-gauge, as good a shotgun as could be had in America at that time. They also gave her a tin of high-grade gunpowder, a gift so unexpected that it was some weeks before she could bring herself to open the can. These gifts changed Annie from being merely a somewhat bohemian wood sprite into a shooter with a future. She repaid their kindness by shipping them game that had been meticulously cleaned and packed—soon they were relaying some of it to high-end restaurants in Cincinnati. With the grocer's encouragement, she soon began to enter shooting matches. She entered and she won.

In the late 1870s such matches abounded. Sharpshooters traveled from town to town and hamlet to hamlet, rather as pool sharks were later to do, eager to take on the local champion and perhaps win a few dollars. The shoots were advertised in the local papers and were commonly well attended, there being little else to be enjoyed in the way of entertainment in the Ohio woods in those days.

Frank Butler was an Irishman with a good deal of confidence in his shooting, but on this occasion, the fact that his opponent was a mere slip of a girl, dressed in knickerbockers, seems to have unnerved him. Annie beat him, hitting twenty-three pigeons to his twenty-one—other accounts say that she only beat him by one bird.

She not only beat him, she won him. The romantic progress of little Phoebe Moses and the dapper Frank Butler is somewhat clouded, but one way or another, there *was* a courtship, followed by a marriage that was to last a lifetime. Exactly when and where they married is disputed. Frank Butler was in the process of getting a divorce—it may be that legal complications caused Annie and Frank to fudge matters a little. They were married in 1882, when Annie was twenty-two; the newlyweds then traveled the variety circuit for some three years, shooting wherever they could find a match, or a weekend's engagement. They were, for a while, a shooting team, but Frank soon dropped into a managerial role, securing bookings and trying to establish his wife in what was a very crowded field. Trick shots and sharpshooters of all stamps were thick on the ground. The young couple stayed in theatrical boardinghouses and traveled as cheaply as possible. They were young, of course, and resilient, but Annie's years as a slave to the "wolves" were not forgotten: to the end of her life it bothered her to turn down work; probably she never fully believed that she could afford to turn down work. Long after her retirement from Cody's show she appeared more than once in Tony Pastor's Opera House, headlining a bill that included Samson, the Strongest Man on Earth, as well as the Ossified Man, whose torso gave back a stony sound when struck with a hammer; beside these attractions there was the Elastic Skin Lady, contortionist extraordinary, a one-armed juggler, and a troop of musicians. It was, in other words, a freak show, but, just to be on the safe side, Annie did the show and banked the money. She had already starred in *The*

Western Girl, a stage melodrama not much better than some of those Bill Cody had once starred in.

By this time, with the glories of Europe behind them and thousands of shows under their belt, Frank Butler might have been inclined to give a real and final farewell performance—a farewell performance that took, unlike Colonel Cody's.

Annie had no very strong objection to Frank's desire for more time to fish and hunt, but her strongest instinct was never to turn down work. Even after her car wreck in 1922 she was not entirely ready to put a period to her career.

4

I N her long life as a performer Annie Oakley is said to have missed only five performances due to illness. Four of these missed shows occurred early in the troupe's stand on Staten Island, after a bug crawled into her ear while she was asleep. Various doctors thought they had flushed the bug, but all failed. For a few days, just as the troupe was girding up for the big opening day parade in Manhattan, Annie Oakley, instead of getting better, got worse. Oils, leeches, everything was tried, but nothing worked—for a time it seemed as if her rival, Lillian Smith, would be in the parade, but not her. Annie had already lopped six years off her age because of this troublesome teenager: the thought that Lillian Smith might upstage her before all New York was too much.

The train carrying most of the troupe had already left, but Annie ordered her horse saddled, changed clothes while this was happening, and raced off to catch the train, which she did. The parade was a long one, but at least she was in it. By the time it ended she was too weak to dismount. Salsbury ordered the best doctors and the ear was finally lanced, but the verdict was blood poisoning. For the next four days, while Buffalo Bill's Wild West packed the ferries and the trains, Annie Oakley lay close to death. But on the fifth day, she showed signs of life and by showtime was ready to perform, although with a heavily bandaged ear.

The long stay on Staten Island left Annie plenty of time in which to develop new acts. Her immediate ambition was fueled by her intense desire to outdo Lillian Smith, the young California sharpshooter whose mere presence on the lot irritated Annie to an extreme. Whatever nice things she said about Cody later, it's not clear that she ever forgave him for bringing Lillian Smith into the troupe.

Lillian Smith was billed as a rapid-fire shooter; she broke innumerable glass balls or plates in quick succession. Insofar as there was a division of labor in this early stage of the show's evolution, Lillian Smith was the rifle shot, Annie Oakley the genius of the shotgun. Annie, who could shoot either weapon proficiently, decided to up the ante by developing acts in which she herself was in motion. She shot while riding a bicycle, and then moved on to horses. Frank was skeptical and Salsbury fearful but Annie soon became an excellent horsewoman. She shot lying full-length on her horse's back, and even learned to shoot standing up on her mount. The fact that she was shooting birdshot out of a smoothbore gun helped a lot when it came to breaking glass balls; but even the great Cody used a smoothbore gun when he shot his glass balls. (Cody and Doc Carver did at first use bullets but the result was too many broken windows from houses several blocks away.)

During this relatively settled period on Staten Island, Cody, Salsbury, and Major Burke had time to give some thought to what lay ahead. They had already committed themselves to go to England and perform at Queen Victoria's Golden Jubilee; they were in the midst of their most successful season ever, and yet Cody already felt the need for more. There were too many shows in the field. Pawnee Bill would soon have a good one up and running, and old Barnum himself was not finished.

Cody's insight, at this juncture, was that mere "combinations," however star-studded, weren't going to satisfy audiences much longer. It was fine to have Annie Oakley and a couple of other sharpshooters; fine to have buffalo, Indians, cowboys, trick ropers, a brass band, and so on. Some of the skits from his own frontier experience—the Pony Express, the attack on the settler's cabin, or the Deadwood stage—were fine skits; they provided the audience with at least a whiff of the Wild West. But Cody wanted more narrative—he always wanted more narrative, even though it would be narrative in its broadest, crudest form.

What he didn't want was a show that was merely an advanced form of rodeo, with the safest acts (like the grand entry) first and the more dangerous acts, like bronc busting, later.

What Cody wanted was a theme; and since he was about to go international, the broader the theme, the better. The concept he came up with, after much brainstorming with Salsbury and Burke, was the broadest theme possible: civilization itself.

At first blush this sounds ridiculous. How could a bunch of poorly educated scouts and actors pretend to enact the drama of the advance of civilization—and yet that is exactly what they proceeded to attempt.

Already, too, Cody was looking to the day when more and more performances would be held indoors, in vast sports palaces, which would protect them from debacles such as the forty-four days of rain in New Orleans. As it happened, a promising venue lay just across the way: Madison Square Garden, where Salsbury had already arranged a short run just before the troupe departed for England.

Already Major Burke's press books were growing longer and more elaborate—the one for the great Chicago Exposition of 1893 would be sixty-four pages long. Buffalo Bill's Wild West was publishing its own history, even as it made it.

By the time the show ended its successful run on Staten Island and prepared to move into town, the new concept under which they all were to labor had been finalized. Buffalo Bill's Wild West would be presenting nothing less ambitious than the Drama of Civilization, beginning deep in the primeval forest and bouncing forward in great leaps.

Where the Drama of Civilization was concerned, Annie Oakley kept her thoughts to herself. Her part in the drama, in any case, was just to keep breaking glass balls. The worst time she had in Manhattan was when the company's pet moose, Jerry, who had been trained to pull a cart, could not resist the smell of a big pile of nice juicy apples on a vendor's stand. The vendor was not pleased to have his stock ravished by a moose—Little Missie had to fork over $5 in order to make peace with the man.

Grandmother England

1

BUFFALO BILL'S Wild West went to England in Queen Victoria's Jubilee year ostensibly to add a little flavor to a big American trade fair, which was already open in Earl's Court, though receiving little attention. It never did garner much attention. The big troupe of wild Westerners soon sucked away what few visitors the trade show had managed to attract. The tail immediately began to wag the dog: the American Exposition was a big flop, and Buffalo Bill's Wild West an enormous success, playing to some two and a half million people before moving on to shorter runs in Manchester and Birmingham. The enormous turnout was still just enough to save Cody and Salsbury's financial bacon due to the expense of the huge troupe they brought over, a full count of which is hard to come by. There were 97 Indians, 160 horses, 16 buffalo, a couple of bears, elk, deer, and of course, scores of performers and stagehands.

Among the Indians making the trip, besides Black Elk and the popular Red Shirt, were Mr. and Mrs. Walking Buffalo, Mr. and Mrs. Eagle Horse, Moccasin Tom, Blue Rainbow, Iron Good Voice, Mr. and Mrs. Cut Meat, and Double Wound, to give only a very abbreviated list. Were this not enough, the bushy-bearded John Y. Nelson managed with his wife to produce a fine papoose along the way, a little boy much appreciated by the royal family. There was also a thirty-six-piece band.

In general the Indians trusted Pahaska (sometimes Pawhaska) Cody, but were nonetheless apprehensive about crossing the Big

Water; going behind the sunrise, as they saw it, could not be a good idea. It was a rough crossing, too; some thought they were doomed— more than one death song floated up from the underdeck. Almost everyone got seasick, though Annie Oakley didn't. There was much rejoicing when the *State of Nebraska* finally reached the Albert Dock. Major Burke, of course, was there ahead of them, doing the same things that press agents do now: securing advertising, setting up interviews, and so forth.

Annie Oakley was soon secure in her snug, nicely carpeted tent—she quickly found that she liked English ways and said more than once that if it had not been for the need to see her old and ailing mother, she would have been well content to make England her home.

Because it was Grandmother England's—the Indians' name for Queen Victoria—Jubilee year, much of the world's royalty (to which, in many cases, she was literally the grandmother) stayed in or at least passed through London while the Wild West was performing. The future Kaiser Wilhelm II was there, as well as Crown Prince Rudolf of Austria, who was soon to die by his own hand in the tragic suicide at Mayerling. Almost everyone loved the show, although there were a few sourpusses, one of them being the poet James Russell Lowell, who had recently been our minister to the Court of St. James. Lowell was much too high-minded for such populist entertainment, attributing the show's immense success to "the dullness of the average English mind."

One night there were no fewer than twenty royals crammed into the royal box, among whom were the four kings who would soon find themselves careering around the arena in the Deadwood stage.

The one person who liked the wildly successful Wild West even less than James Russell Lowell was George Sanger, head of the largest and best-established English circus company, from whom Cody drained spectators as easily as he had from the big trade fair. Indeed, throughout the whole six-month run there was hardly a day when Cody's name did not appear in the London newspapers, where he was usually referred to as the Honorable William F. Cody. Aware that the English might be picky about titles, Cody had come prepared with a sheaf of testimonials from many military men; he had even persuaded the governor of Nebraska to make him a colonel, though exactly what unit he was supposed to be colonel of was not easy to say.

George Sanger was so annoyed at constantly seeing Cody referred to as "the Honorable" that he summarily added an "Honorable" to his own name.

Very fortunately for Mr. Sanger, Queen Victoria, upon being informed of George Sanger's aggressive act, decided in this instance to be amused.

2

FROM the viewpoint of the Honorable George Sanger, the circumstance that most added insult to injury where Cody was concerned, was the fact the one person who did the most to siphon customers to Buffalo Bill's Wild West was his own sovereign, Queen Victoria. Major John Burke could have labored in the English pressrooms for years without securing as much good publicity for the show as the queen did merely by agreeing to attend.

Queen Victoria's appearance at their London show was the greatest stroke of luck Cody and Salsbury were to have on any of their European outings. Grandmother England to the Indians, she was, as I have said, literally grandmother to most of the sitting royalty of Europe. Both the soon-to-be Kaiser Wilhelm II of Germany and the soon-enough-to-be Tsar Nicholas II of Russia were her grandsons, and there were many more grandchildren scattered through lesser duchies and states.

What made Victoria's appearance at a command performance in Earl's Court so extraordinary was that she had remained in mourning for twenty-six of her fifty years as queen—in mourning for her beloved husband, Albert. Until Cody and the Wild West came along, if the queen wanted to see a play or a revue, the players came to her, usually at Windsor Castle, where they performed in her own theater.

And in fact, she would have had the Wild West perform at Windsor had she not been persuaded that it would be physically impossible to have so many animals running around the castle. The buffalo might abscond, as they once had from P. T. Barnum on Staten Island.

What probably whetted the queen's curiosity to an intolerable pitch was gossip that floated back to her from the two command performances that preceded hers, one ordered by Prime Minister Gladstone and the other by her own son, the often disappointing Albert Edward, Prince of Wales, by whom she was very seldom amused though frequently annoyed because of the prince's gambling or philandering activities that were sure, sooner or later, to embarrass the throne. No one would ever defend more seriously the dignity of that particular throne than the small plump lady who sat on it from 1837 until her death, in 1901.

The first command performance, for the prime minister, went off rockingly, after which Cody, Annie Oakley, Red Shirt, Lillian Smith, and others came up to be presented to the Prince of Wales and his shy, gentle wife, the long-suffering Princess Alexandra. When it became Annie Oakley's turn to shake, or at least touch, hands with the royal couple, Annie boldly dispensed with protocol and shook the princess's hand first. "I'm sorry," she said to the startled prince, whose hand she then shook. "I'm an American and in America ladies come first."

Annie Oakley's shooting act was wildly successful in London, so successful that no one much wanted to comment on this gaffe. Although a mature woman of twenty-seven at the time, she still looked like a slip of a girl. No one wanted to be harsh, so the slip was put down to girlish naivete, when in fact it was probably the one purely feminist act of Annie Oakley's life. Annie knew—because everyone knew—that the Prince of Wales was a shameless and, indeed, a serial philanderer. The gentle Alexandra was much beloved, and not least because of the grace with which she ignored, to the extent that was possible, the prince's terrible behavior. Annie Oakley did what she did in order to show support for a sister of a sort. Whether Princess Alexandra understood this is unclear, but she did love the Wild West and, as I mentioned earlier, once slipped incognito into the press box in order to watch it without herself being quite so onstage.

* * *

Buffalo Bill Cody got along splendidly with the Prince of Wales, with whom he shared many faults. Cody saw the prince as a man he could happily drink with, carouse with, shoot with, club with. Throughout the show's run the prince frequently invited Cody here and there, and Cody usually went. One or two aristos may have snubbed Cody, or at least have maintained a stiff formality; but Cody, as usual, was too affable and too presentable to be kept out.

When Queen Victoria showed up for her command performance, or later, when she summoned the troupe to Windsor for tea and a visit, she was not rude to Cody but she also made no effort to single him out for attention. She told Annie Oakley that she was "a very clever little girl" and she definitely admired Red Shirt's good looks. It may be that she saw in Cody a man whose habits were too much like her eldest son's.

3

THERE are numerous printed accounts of Queen Victoria's visit to Buffalo Bill's Wild West—she herself twice recorded her admiration for Red Shirt and her surprise that the Indians, mainly Sioux, were so good-looking. The visit was mentioned in many memoirs and picked up by so many newspapers that Louisa Cody heard about it and concluded that both Queen Victoria and Princess Alexandra had paid improper attentions to her husband. Bitterness over the queen's visit surfaced eighteen years after the fact, in the ill-conceived and unsuccessful divorce attempt that Cody pressed in 1905.

Of the many accounts of the earth-shattering visit of the queen, who had been absent from the public eye for twenty-six years, the most poetic and most charming by far is that of Nicholas Black Elk, the young Ogalala who had been coaxed into coming on the trip because he was the best dancer the Sioux could boast.

In Black Elk's account, "Grandmother England" arrived in "a big shining wagon with soldiers on both sides."

Black Elk and his friends proceeded to dance themselves silly:

We stood right in front of Grandmother England. She was little but fat, and we liked her because she was good to us. After we danced she spoke to us. She said "I am sixty-seven years old . . . I have seen all kinds of people; but today I have seen the best looking people I know. If you belonged to me, I would not let them take you around in a show like this."

We all shook hands with her. Her hand was very little and soft. We gave a big cheer for her and then the shining wagons came in and she got into one of them and they all went away.

Then, Windsor:

. . . in about half a moon we went to see Grandmother. They put us into some of those shining wagons and took us . . . to a very big house with sharp pointed towers on it. There were many seats built high in a circle, and these were just full of Wasichus [whites] who were all pounding their heels and yelling: Jubilee! Jubilee! Jubilee! I never heard what this meant.

Then we saw Grandmother England again . . . Her dress was all shining and her hat was all shining and her wagon was all shining and so were the horses. She looked like a fire coming . . .

We sent up a great cry and our women made the tremolo . . . when it was quiet we sang a song to the Grandmother . . .

We liked Grandmother because we could see that she was a good woman, and she was good to us. Maybe if she had been our grandmother it would have been better for our people.

4

WHEN the long run at Earl's Court ended, the troupe loaded up and played Birmingham and then Manchester, after which they sailed for home, with young Nicholas Black Elk not among them. Always curious, and habituated to running on his own notion of time, rather than the playbill's, he somehow failed to make the disembarkment and was wandering around Manchester when he bumped into some other Indians who were similarly stranded. Fortunately they were all to some extent show people now; they soon managed to get on with an impresario named Mexican Joe whose troupe was then performing in London. Mexican Joe didn't have many Indians; he was glad to take them on at a wage of $1 a day.

When Mexican Joe moved on to Paris he took the Indians with him. Black Elk was particularly wary of the Metro—he didn't like the sight of people disappearing into the ground.

Black Elk got very sick in Paris. The Indians who were with him decided he was a goner and went out to make a coffin; but Black Elk recovered and was taken in by his French girlfriend for the rest of his stay. While lying near death in her Paris apartment, Black Elk had one of his greatest visions: the vision of the cloud that came to take him home.

Then I was alone on the cloud, and it was going fast, I clung to it hard because I was afraid I might fall off. Far down below I could see houses and towns and green land and streams, and it all looked flat.

Then I was right over the big water. I was not afraid any more, because, by now, I knew I was going home. It was dark and then it was light again, and I could see a big town below me, and I knew it was the one where we first got on the big fireboat, and that I was in my own country again. The cloud and I kept going very fast, and I could see streams and towns and green lands. Then I began to recognize the country below me. I saw the Missouri River. Then I saw far off the Black Hills and the center of the world where the spirits had taken me in my great vision.

Then I was right over Pine Ridge, and the cloud stopped and I looked down and could not understand what I saw, because it seemed that nearly all my people were gathered together there in a big camp. I saw my father and mother's teepee. They were outside and she was cooking. I wanted to jump off the cloud and be with them, but I was afraid it would kill me. While I was looking down my mother looked up, and I felt sure she saw me. But just then the cloud started going back, very fast . . . I was very sad, but I could not get off . . . soon the cloud and I were going right back over the big town again, then there was only water underneath me, and the night came without stars; and I was all alone in a black world and I was crying. But after a while some light began to peep in far ahead of me. Then I saw earth beneath me and towns and green land and houses, all flying backward. Soon the cloud stopped over a big town, and a house began to come up toward me, turning round as it came. When it touched the cloud it caught me and began to drop down, turning round and round with me.

It touched the ground and I heard the girl's voice.

Soon after Black Elk recovered, Cody arrived in Paris on his first continental tour. Black Elk soon found his way to him. Cody offered him a job, but he soon saw that Black Elk was too homesick to be much use. With his usual generosity Cody got him a berth home and gave him $90 to see him through to Dakota. It was because of this kind act that Black Elk said Cody had a strong heart.

Cody's European tour of 1889 will be dealt with later. Both he and Black Elk were to be in Dakota again. Cody was blocked in his final attempt to see and possibly soothe Sitting Bull, and Black Elk lived to deliver the saddest statement about the unnecessary tragedy of Wounded Knee.

Before we get to that sad day I would like to finish the account of the triumphs of the Colonel and Little Missie in London—the home of Grandmother England.

5

ALTHOUGH Annie Oakley was outshot a couple of times on her first acquaintance with English shooting, in the main she went, as always, from triumph to triumph and garnered as much good publicity as anyone except Cody himself. Both of them were constantly in the news, with Cody being feted by the biggest wigs in the land. At one point he returned the favor and held a buffalo roast, which greatly pleased all who were invited. The Indians cooked the buffalo and ate their part with their hands—a tiny but vivid illustration of the drama of civilization, which most spectators felt free to ignore. What they liked was the riding and the whooping.

On one shoot at least Annie, boasting the new light gun that Charles Lancaster had crafted for her, scored a triumph over both her archrival, Lillian Smith, and her boss, Bill Cody. This was held at the famous Wimbledon sporting club, which featured a mechanical deer which raced along on a track.

In this era most shooting clubs were, of course, all-male institutions. In many cases Annie Oakley was the first female to set foot in them, and famous though she was, her presence in this rigidly male precinct did not please all members. There were many snubs, both in America and England, and the snubs continued throughout her long career. Annie did her best to ignore them. She stood on her considerable dignity and her even more considerable abilities with the gun.

Lillian Smith also got invitations to shoot and accepted some of them. Probably the reason she didn't accept more was because it was painfully clear that even though she might win the shooting, Annie would inevitably win the crowd.

By the time of the Wimbledon shoot Lillian Smith was under attack in the press; a skeptical English journalist named Carter studied her act through binoculars and accused her of cheating. Most trick shooters cut a corner here and there. Sights that were supposedly covered might not in fact *be* covered. The matter of Lillian Smith's cheating filled the shooting papers for some time, inconclusively. What hurt her more than these accusations was her racy dress. When she arrived at the Wimbledon sporting club she wore a dress that sported a vivid yellow sash, and a plug hat the likes of which had never been seen in this august club before.

The sash and the hat might have been overlooked had Lillian shot well, but she didn't. She twice missed the running deer outright, and then only managed to hit it in the haunch, which, in English eyes, was worse than missing. Members who hit the haunch were in fact fined, since a haunch hit meant a wounded deer.

Lillian Smith tried to make light of the matter, claiming she had brought too heavy a rifle—she agreed to come back, more effectively equipped, and she readily agreed to pay the fine.

In fact, she did neither, annoying the directors of the Wimbledon sporting club no end.

Even more annoying to them was the fact that Buffalo Bill Cody never showed up to shoot at all. Annie was very popular, but Cody was still the headliner and one of the most popular men on earth. Though he may have gone on a few toots while in London, he never neglected his appearance, and his fame was as high as it was possible for fame to be. Why he never showed up to shoot at the mechanical deer has never been explained; probably he was just too busy. It seems unlikely that he doubted his shooting; in real life he had hit more than one running deer.

Cody didn't come, but Annie did. She hit the deer readily, and not in the haunch, either. It was perhaps her most conspicuous triumph over Lillian Smith.

Shortly after this well-publicized shoot there was an attack on Annie, a critique published somewhat remotely, in a California journal called *Breeder and Stockman*. Remote as this calumny seemed to be—some thought it had been commissioned by Lillian Smith—Nate Salsbury and Frank Butler took it very seriously—any threat to Annie's credibility as a markswoman must be taken seriously by those running the show. Salsbury knew how much the show needed Annie Oakley—her ability to draw crowds was exceeded only by Cody's. (In France, as we shall see, she was *more* of a draw than Cody, at least at first.)

Frank Butler wrote a long rebuttal to the piece in the *Breeder and Stockman*. Most thought that he had successfully defended his wife's reputation.

Then, just as the troupe was ready to pack up and head for Birmingham, Annie Oakley and Frank Butler made a decision that rocked Nate Salsbury, even though he may have seen it coming. The couple quietly quit the show and made their way back to New York.

6

EXACTLY why Annie Oakley and her manager-husband decided to take herself out of Buffalo Bill's Wild West at this juncture will probably never be known—at least not in full. There had always been rumblings and occasional disagreements with Cody, but no more serious rumblings than could be expected of any star performer amid the pressures of an extended run.

What Annie claimed, in her little eulogy to Cody on the occasion of his death—that she had never had a contract with him—was as big a lie as her instinctive lie about her age. She had many contracts with Cody's Wild West, all of them meticulously negotiated by Frank Butler. In these contracts it was clearly stated that Annie had the right to do considerable shooting on her own. She could give exhibitions and enter shooting competitions; she did both and made good money at it, sometimes as much as $750 a week, big money indeed for that day and time.

At one point she received an excellent offer to compete in Germany, and she meant to accept, but Salsbury seems to have blocked it by insisting that he couldn't do without his star for that long. Or Cody may have grumbled. At this point Annie and Frank had been with the Wild West a little more than three years, during which time Annie's fame had steadily risen. She wanted to shoot in Germany and eventually did.

I doubt, myself, that Cody was jealous of the attention Annie got in the London papers. The attention brought in more customers, and in any case, he got more publicity and was still the bigger star.

I don't think there's any need to claim that the Butlers' break with the show posited some huge falling-out between themselves and management—that is, Cody and Salsbury. Nowhere in the numerous biographies is there much indication that the Butlers and Cody were really close friends. They were star performers, working together in a show—possibly there were tiffs, but when aren't there tiffs? Cody was gregarious and outgoing; he liked to drink and carouse and had an abundance of opportunities to do so in the great world capital where he found himself.

Annie Oakley, by contrast, was very private. Her spirits during this run seemed to have been high, but that didn't mean she was out with the boys, slugging them down. She stayed in her tent and did her needlework. Frank may have slipped his lead now and then, but not very seriously. As far as dissipation went Annie might occasionally allow herself a glass of beer, particularly if someone else was paying.

Annie's intense dislike of Lillian Smith may have been a big part of the reason she and Frank left the Wild West at this time. Or it could merely have been that the Butlers felt they could do better financially on their own.

Cody, for his part, may have reasoned that the Wild West was now so well established that even the loss of a big star would not really affect the box office that much.

The shift to independence seemed to have proved, for the Butlers, mildly disappointing. They easily got bookings, but much travel was involved and $750 weeks were few and far between. They more than held their own but freelancing soon proved to be quite a bit harder than working for Cody.

When the likable Gordon Lillie (Pawnee Bill) offered to hire them for a short tour they readily accepted and the tour did well, a fact that Cody and Salsbury, back in New York by then, certainly noticed. The Wild West was preparing for a big tour of Europe in 1889 and both men realized that after all, they still needed Annie Oakley. She was a bigger star than anyone except Cody himself.

For their part, it probably didn't take the Butlers long to figure out that they functioned better as part of an established troupe. Cody and Salsbury offered the best environment; with them, Annie—shooting maybe twenty minutes a day—could remain a major superstar. The transportation would be arranged for them, and they didn't have to carry their own instruments, as it were. Besides that, Annie could profit from the energetic talents of Major Burke, a man Annie came to like, although she was not as deeply fond of him as Louisa Cody seemed to be.

In any case the Butlers soon sat down with Salsbury and ironed out whatever differences there may have been. Annie Oakley happily came back to Buffalo Bill's Wild West. Not until the traumatic train wreck in 1903 would she leave it again.

When Annie returned, Lillian Smith resigned. The two sharpshooters would rarely cross paths again.

7

THE tour of Europe which Cody and Salsbury plunged into in 1889 was as ambitious as any season they would ever mount. In Paris, where they had a seven-month run, the importance of having Annie Oakley in the troupe was quickly demonstrated. The first show came very close to being a flop, the French remaining true to their reputation of being hard to get. The crowd seemed glacially indifferent to Cody, cowboys, buffalos, broncos, Indians, ropers, and the thirty-six-piece band. It was clearly the wrong place to speak of the Drama of Civilization, since the French *were* civilization, at least in their eyes.

At first they were wholly reluctant to clap for anything they were seeing.

Sensing disaster, Salsbury rushed Annie into the arena and she immediately saved the day, riding and shooting so brilliantly that the crowd leapt to its feet and in the end called her back for six encores. Once the show got established the French quickly acquired a strong yen for Indian souvenirs: moccasins, baskets, and bows sold in great numbers.

The Wild West eventually went on to Barcelona, Naples, Rome, Florence, Bologna, Milan, and Venice, where Indians in full warbonnets were photographed on the Grand Canal. They then played Vienna, took a little trip on the Danube, and went into winter quarters in Benfield. It was in Naples that Major Burke was briefly fired.

For this second tour over the waters Cody and Salsbury took

seventy-two Indians from Pine Ridge, five of whom died during the tour. Two men, Lone Wolf and Star, are buried in Brompton Cemetery, London.

These deaths, which the Indians said were to be expected, were nonetheless noted by the authorities at home. In Berlin two U.S. consuls came and inspected conditions; both reported that they had never seen Indians looking so well-fed and so healthy.

Still, there were complaints from America, both from within the government and out, a problem Cody and Salsbury took very seriously. If they were denied Indians the whole tour would be compromised. Salsbury stayed in Europe to keep things in good order, and Cody went home, taking some of the Indians with him.

8

BILL CODY'S oblique and frustrating near involvement with the Ghost Dance crisis on the Dakota reservations in December of 1890 is perhaps the oddest thing that happened to him during his long career, as first a fighter of, and then an employer of, Indians.

For the now essentially captive Sioux, the decade of the 1880s had been one long disappointment. With the exceptions of Sitting Bull and Red Cloud their major leaders were dead. More and more white settlers poured into the northern plains, the result being that the Sioux had to watch their reservations being constantly whittled down. They were repeatedly asked to make do with less; the buffalo were gone, they were dependent on agency beef, they had no work and were in an increasingly dismal situation.

Sitting Bull was at the Standing Rock reservation, living quietly and occasionally riding the show horse that Buffalo Bill had given him. The fine sombrero he kept mainly for ceremonial occasions.

Sitting Bull, when possible, avoided conflict with Agent James McLaughlin, who administered the Pine Ridge agency. Throughout the reservation system complaints about the slow and puny food allotments were constant. The beeves that the Indians depended on were usually slow in arriving, and were usually too few in number.

Indeed, the Pine Ridge and Standing Rock reservations were wretched places to be, as they still are. With the buffalo gone, an old and established life way was destroyed. The general wretchedness and drunkenness made it easy for Cody to get Indians to sign up for his shows. It was better than staying home and being depressed.

Agent McLaughlin and other honest administrators knew that the Indians were miserable. They worried that somehow there might yet be an outbreak and they overreacted to the slightest sign of independence among the bands. Their response to the Ghost Dance was just such an overreaction. Though it must have been obvious that the Sioux lacked the arms and the leadership necessary to any sort of sustained revolt, the arrival of the Ghost Dance somehow tipped the balance. Worry became paranoia.

Native American millenarianism was hardly a new thing—Native American prophets began to preach against the whites as early as the sixteenth century; they predicted that the whites would vanish, the dead return, and the world be restored to the condition it had been in before the whites arrived.

Many prophets preached some version of a Return story, in which the Native American world would regain its old fullness. In the late nineteenth century these prophets mostly emerged from the desert places. In 1881 an Apache preacher named Noch-ay-del-klinne was killed, with a number of his followers, on Cibicue Creek, in Arizona. He too preached of the Return, a powerful idea that gave hope to an essentially powerless people.

The prophet most associated with the flourishing of the Ghost Dance was a short fat Paiute named Wovoka, whose white name was Jack Wilson. He lived mostly with a white family in Nevada. When Indian leaders from far away—Kansas, Oklahoma—wanted to learn about the Ghost Dance they came to Jack Wilson for instruction. He left a few instructional texts—Messiah letters, these were called—about how to perform the dance and what to expect. There was no call to violence in the letters or in his preaching. The Ghost Dance was a long dance that brought the dancers to a state of spiritual purification. Jack Wilson goes out of his way to warn the dancers to leave the whites alone. The dancers were merely to dance for a long time, then bathe in the creek and stay with their families.

Nonetheless, thanks to the long history of plains warfare, the white administrators were simply unable to take a calm view of sizable groups of Indians assembling for any purpose at all. The whole reservation system had been designed to separate tribe from tribe and lessen the risks that they associated with large assemblies.

Agent McLaughlin was unhappy when the Ghost Dance arrived at Pine Ridge, but for a time at least, he tried to maintain perspective. In several dispatches he mentions that the Sioux were behaving well. Above all, he hoped to keep the army out; the army had a way of making things worse.

McLaughlin's relationship with Sitting Bull had been touchy, but so far not catastrophic. At one point he went to visit the old Hunkpapa to express his concern about the Ghost Dance, his fear being that the young warriors would get so stirred up by the dancing that they might go back to killing whites. Sitting Bull seems to have genuinely tried to mollify McLaughlin. It is just some people dancing, he said—it was nothing to be alarmed about. Then he made McLaughlin an unusual offer, so some authorities say. He himself didn't put much stock in preachers or Messiahs, but if McLaughlin was so worried about this man Wovoka, perhaps the two of them ought to pay him a visit. If they found him and he was indeed a Messiah then they could determine what his disposition was. But if Wovoka failed to convince, then Sitting Bull could tell his people that the Ghost Dance was all hooey. It wasn't going to bring the buffalo back, or cause a new earth to rise, or raise the dead, or drive the whites away.

If this offer was made Agent McLaughlin would have done well to take it, but he didn't. No doubt he feared to leave his agency at such a nervous time.

Meanwhile, in New York, Buffalo Bill Cody, indignant about the charges that he had mistreated Indians, was prepared to go to Washington with a number of Indians to refute these charges. Of course, with several troupes in Europe, all of them employing Indians, some abuse may have occurred, but most of the complaints usually boiled down to seasickness. None of the Indians enjoyed crossing the great water.

Before Cody could get his group on the train to Washington, he received a bolt from the blue, in the form of a succinct telegram from General Nelson A. Miles, whom he had known for some time. It read:

> Col. Cody,
> You are authorized to secure the person of Sitting Bull and . . . deliver him to the nearest com'g officer of US troops, taking a receipt and reporting your action.
>
> Nelson A. Miles

On the back Miles had scribbled a note assuring Cody that the army would offer him all the assistance he needed.

Cody had just returned from a long stay in Europe. Whether he knew of the Ghost Dance excitement I'm not sure, but to receive an order from a major general asking him to proceed to the very heart of Sioux country and summarily arrest their leader in the midst of his people could only have come as a major shock.

It was no less a shock to Agent McLaughlin, when he received a copy. For Cody or anybody else to ride into Standing Rock and arrest Sitting Bull would very likely mean bloodshed and probably provoke the revolt McLaughlin was trying so hard to prevent.

Agent McLaughlin immediately got on the singing wires, telegraphing everyone he could think of to assure them that the situation was peaceful at Standing Rock. He insisted that there was no immediate threat—if it eventually seemed necessary to arrest Sitting Bull, then native policemen could probably handle the arrest without bloodshed.

Buffalo Bill Cody McLaughlin distinctly did *not* need—but the man was already on the way. The military and the administrators had got their wires crossed. General Miles continued to insist that Cody was their best bet, but by the time Cody actually reached South Dakota various official barricades had been thrown up. Cody saw General Miles but never got close to Sitting Bull—in hindsight it's hard not to think that McLaughlin used bad judgment here. Sitting Bull knew that Cody had friendly feelings for him—if Cody had been permitted to see his old star it is not likely that he would have tried to arrest him, but it might have defused the tense situation.

Cody had come a long way for nothing and was more than a little annoyed. He went down to his home in North Platte, though not before he secured a few fresh Indians from Pine Ridge for his show.

A few days before Sitting Bull's death, legend has it, he was taking a walk and minding his own business when a cheeky meadowlark, speaking in Sioux, informed him that he would soon be killed by his own people. Sitting Bull probably wished the meadowlark, too, had minded his own business; but the prophecy soon came true. McLaughlin sent a troop of native policemen to ask Sitting Bull to come to the agency, a request he usually complied with, though with much grumbling. The native policemen arrived early, hoping to get Sitting Bull out before the camp was well awake. They were early, but not early enough. Sitting Bull started to submit, but changed his mind when he saw that quite a few Ghost Dancers had lined up to support him. A scuffle ensued: two native policemen, Bull Head and Red Tomahawk, both shot Sitting Bull, who died on the spot, along with one of his sons and several others. Had the army not thoughtfully provided a sizable backup force all the native policemen would very likely have been killed.

Cody was out of the way well before this happened. He would have seen nothing wrong about visiting his old friend Sitting Bull; the two might have had a good powwow, but it is unlikely he would have said anything about turning him over to the army. His show depended in good measure on the goodwill of the Sioux, which he would have quickly lost if he had tried to arrest Sitting Bull. General Miles's simple hope seems to have been that Cody could lure him away from the reservation with the promise of medals or something, after which the army could have taken over.

It may be that, once he was in striking distance, some officer told him that Sitting Bull was already on his way to Pine Ridge, using a different road. Cody was relaxing in North Platte when he learned of Sitting Bull's death.

The death of their toughest chief threw all the northern Sioux into confusion. They expected big trouble to result, and big trouble did result, although not immediately. Sitting Bull was killed on the fifteenth of December 1889. Because six native policemen had died in the struggle to arrest him, the Sioux expected reprisals—many fled to the hills, while others made their way to the comparative safety of the Pine Ridge agency.

Among the groups headed for Pine Ridge were the people led by Chief Big Foot, who was ill with pneumonia at the time. Indeed, he was so ill that the officer who took charge of this group immediately ordered him a doctor and a heated tent as well. This occurred near Wounded Knee Creek, not far east of Pine Ridge.

The next morning, with a large contingent of the Seventh Cavalry standing by, an attempt was made to disarm the Indians in Big Foot's camp. The attempt was hurried and rough. The exact sequence of events which led to the massacre has been debated ever since; but at some point the soldiers began to shoot the Indians and the Indians fought back with knives, hatchets, and small arms. A massacre occurred, Big Foot was immediately killed, as were a total of 146 Sioux, many of them women and children. So desperately did the Sioux fight that twenty-five soldiers also died; nearly forty more were hurt.

Nicholas Black Elk, looking over the carnage of this battle, left the most elegant statement that we have about the tragedy of Wounded Knee:

And so it was all over.

I did not know then how much was ended. When I look back from this high hill of my old age, I can still see the butchered women and the children lying heaped and scattered all along the crooked gulch as plain as when I saw them with eyes still young. And I can see that something else died there in the bloody mud, and was buried in the blizzard. A people's dream died there. It was a beautiful dream.

And I, to whom so great a vision was given in my youth, you see me now a pitiful old man who has done nothing, for the nation's hoop is broken and scattered. There is no center anymore, and the sacred tree is dead.

Buffalo Bill was so annoyed by the poor use the army had made of him that he billed them some $500 for expenses on his unnecessary trip.

Though the Sioux were essentially finished, a brief revolt did flare up. It lasted about two weeks. Cody left North Platte and became a kind of roving liaison man, his main task being to persuade terrified Nebraskans that they need not flee south. Some fled anyway. By the sixteenth of January the last miscreants had given up and the last Sioux outbreak was over. Eleven thousand soldiers were there to assure the surrender.

By this time Major Burke was in Pine Ridge himself—he was escorting some fifty of the Indians who had been in the show back to the place he was supposed to return them.

What Cody really thought about this sad debacle is not easy to say. The film he later made about it no longer exists, of which more later. Perhaps Cody unburdened himself to Major Burke, or Salsbury, or even his wife, but he said nothing disrespectful about the military to any of the reporters who pursued him.

From this distance in time it seems that both General Miles and Agent McLaughlin lost their heads. McLaughlin had visited Sitting Bull only two weeks earlier; the old man may have grumbled, but there was no violence, no threat. Cody was a friend; he might have helped, but the left hand ignored the right hand and the blood of another two hundred people stained the much-stained northern plains.

There was to be one more irony: when the Sioux surrendered in January 1890, they allowed the whites to take nineteen hostages. For their part in the last Sioux revolt they were consigned, by way of punishment, to Buffalo Bill Cody, who had been cleared of all charges relating to abuse.

A short time later the nineteen Sioux were performing in Europe.

The sharpshooter Johnny Baker, whom Annie Oakley mothered and Cody helped raise.

Lillian Smith, Annie Oakley's great rival.

Will Rogers.

Ned Buntline, dime novelist and impresario.

21

22

Doc Carver, Cody's persistent rival.

Gordon Lillie, Pawnee Bill.

Buffalo Bill with his sometime
partner Pawnee Bill.

25

Katherine Clemmons, the actress who was Cody's most expensive mistake.

John Y. Nelson who rode shotgun on the Deadwood stage when it held four kings and a crown prince.

26

*Queen Victoria, who
came out of mourning
to take in the
Wild West.*

Red Shirt, Ogalala much admired by Queen Victoria.

The Grand Duke Alexis of Russia, an exceptionally poor shot.

Spotted Tail, leader of the Brule Sioux and (probably) Crazy Horse's uncle.

The Deadwood stage. On top is John Y. Nelson with two of his children.

One of the railroad cars that carried the Wild West into as many as 130 cities a year.

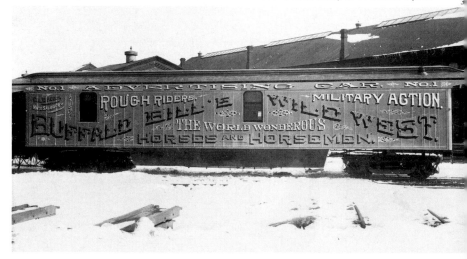

9

THERE is debate about the origins of the term "Rough Rider." On big ranches half-broken horses were referred to as the "rough string," and the cowboys whose job it was to improve their behavior might have been called "rough riders." It seems clear that Cody and Salsbury used it before Theodore Roosevelt appropriated it for his Cuban campaign. By 1893 Cody's show was grandly called Buffalo Bill's Wild West and Congress of Rough Riders of the World—by this time Salsbury had added gauchos, Cossacks, vaqueros, and Arabs to the mix.

Salsbury was in Europe while Cody was in the Dakotas. Though the abuse accusations were easily settled, Salsbury, looking far ahead, decided that it would be wise to slowly shift the emphasis of the show from historical skits to horsemanship. Cody could never have been weaned entirely from his beloved skits, but he was an exceptional horseman himself and would never object to more riders.

The 1891 tour through northern Europe involved ten stops in Germany alone, with only occasional mishaps or alarums. One occurred while Annie Oakley was giving shooting lessons to a Bavarian prince—a horse broke loose and came charging their way, forcing Annie to wrestle the startled prince to the ground.

Kaiser Wilhelm saw her shoot a cigarette out of her husband's mouth and demanded that she try it with him, which she did, though she didn't like the Kaiser and later remarked that he was just the sort of man who would start a war. After he had, she informed him that if they ever tried the trick again she could not guarantee the results.

Needless to say, they never tried the trick again. Her appraisal of the Kaiser shows how quickly and accurately the young woman from Darke County, Ohio, could size up people—particularly the great and famous. Bismarck, she remarked, looked like a mastiff. Throughout their travels together she exhibited far less tolerance than Cody for the company of stuffed shirts—though she did give shooting lessons to a good many of them, and to their children as well.

The 1891 tour boasted the show's most swollen roster, with 640 "eating members"—and eating members ate three full meals a day, an arrangement that the Indians found very satisfactory.

Grandmother England came to the Wild West again and was particularly pleased that Cody had added Cossacks to the roster. Cody was again presented to the queen. He was on the wagon that summer, under strict orders from Salsbury to indulge in no more toots. When offered drinks by the queen's equerry Cody staunchly refused; Salsbury merely accepted a glass of wine. Cody's abstinence drew favorable notices from the Salvation Army and the temperance societies.

In an unusual ceremony in Manchester, the nineteen survivors of the Charge of the Light Brigade were honored. Not mentioned, but also present, were nineteen survivors of the Battle of Wounded Knee.

10

B Y 1893 Buffalo Bill's Wild West had put behind them a number of successful runs, with the show on Staten Island and their appearance at the Golden Jubilee being among the best. Millions saw the show on its European runs, and more millions saw it in America. But nothing Cody or Salsbury had done or would ever do surpassed their success at the World's Columbian Exposition in Chicago in 1893.

Salsbury, unable to get adequate space inside the exposition grounds, wisely rented two large lots right across from the main entrance to the fair itself. So vast was the scale of this exposition, one of the most successful in history, that many people probably wandered into the Wild West thinking they were seeing the fair itself: many of them spent all their money with Cody and Salsbury and never caught the real fair across the street.

The great Chicago Columbian Exposition was open from May until the end of October, and some 27,500,000 people poured through the gates; an amazing 716,000 paid admission on one day, October 9. Major Burke saw to it that Cody was constantly in the papers. Cody was the only private citizen to join two thousand legislators and watch President Grover Cleveland push a button and turn on the lights to get the exposition going.

With time to spare, Major Burke outdid himself, producing a lavishly illustrated sixty-four-page booklet which didn't stint in its praise, calling the show:

The biggest outdoor animated amusement exploit extant or known either ancient or modern. Life, action, skill, daring, danger defied; one thousand animated pictures in two hours given by flesh and blood; creation's greatest handiwork, nature's noblest mechanism too natural and colossal for canvas or building. The greensward our carpet, heaven's blue canopy our covering . . . an affair of magnitude, second to none in novel entertainment enjoyment, instruction, interest and educative merit.

Cody had insisted on one major change in the standard program: for the ever-popular Attack on the Settler's Cabin he substituted the even more popular Battle of the Little Bighorn, which became the show's finale. Once again Cody was acutely exploiting—as he had with the scalping of Yellow Hair—the tragic fate of the erratic general whom he had, so long ago, guided across the plains.

Annie Oakley's wildly popular shooting act came second on the program, right after the Grand Entry of the Rough Riders of the World. She too was feted in Chicago, but not as much as Cody.

Since the big exposition attracted scores of celebrities, Major Burke devised foolproof techniques for getting them over to the Wild West to have their pictures taken. Among those so snatched was the maharajah of Kapurthala and Frédéric Bartholdi, the sculptor of the Statue of Liberty.

In Chicago Burke and Salsbury saw a way to get the Wild West favorable publicity by organizing the occasional charity performance. Cody liked children—at least he liked them in short stretches—and was often photographed beaming on several in a grandfatherly way. Soon his hair would begin to turn and he would have to consent to wigs, but in Chicago he was a fine-looking man of forty-seven. Someone had the idea of having a "poor children's day" at the exposition, a good idea vetoed by the fair's manager, Harlow Higinbotham, who feared the sight of ten thousand grubby waifs might put off paying customers.

Cody, Salsbury, and Burke at once leapt into this breach, readily paying for a picnic, a parade, and a day at Buffalo Bill's Wild West for poor children from no less than seven orphanages and homes. The publicity that resulted was music to Major Burke's ears:

> Colonel Cody is a true philanthropist. He does not distribute tracts, but sandwiches; he does not inculcate any high moral lessons, but he smooths the rugged pathway of the children of the streets for at least one day by taking them away from their squalid surroundings. So, too, shall Colonel Cody's trail toward the happy hunting grounds be made easy and fringed with prairie flowers because he has done this much to lighten the lives of others.

From Chicago a great lesson was learned; after that, charity days for poor children were to be a regular feature of Buffalo Bill's Wild West.

The one event that didn't quite work out as planned was the thousand-mile horse race from Chadron, Nebraska, to Chicago. Cody, having himself ridden a 322-mile Pony Express run, initially saw nothing wrong with a thousand-mile horse race; but very soon, every form of animal protection society then extant was on his back. Major Burke was forced to issue a number of exculpatory leaflets, pointing out that Buffalo Bill was a charter member of the Humane Society and that he had also been among the first to lobby for the use of clay pigeons rather than live birds in pigeon shoots.

Nonetheless, five horses finished and a rancher from Chadron took home the big first prize.

So far as Rough Riders went, Cody pulled out all stops for the Chicago run. Besides the Cossacks, gauchos, and vaqueros, he added Syrian and Arabian horsemen. He also hired the great trick roper Vincente Orapeza, who became the teacher of Will Rogers.

Also, the Indians were resplendent. John Y. Nelson was still on hand, with his many half-Sioux children. Two tiny survivors of Wounded Knee were there, one of whom, Little No Neck, Major Burke commendably adopted. The very respected Sioux leader Young Man Afraid of His Horses was there, and Red Cloud's son Jack.

It may be that the Chicago run in 1893 was the high-water mark for Buffalo Bill's Wild West. The success was due partly to location and partly to advertising. Swollen as the troupe was, this stand made money—estimates are that Cody and Salsbury cleared close to a million dollars.

Encouraged by this great box office, and concluding, perhaps, that their longer runs were their most successful, they decided to go back to New York, add a few attractions, and hope the crowds would come.

This time they chose south Brooklyn, where there was ample space. Salsbury no longer wanted to be vulnerable to the vagaries of the weather, so a covered grandstand was built. Major Burke kicked up as much publicity as he could and the shows ran twice a day, admission fifty cents.

But to the shock of the owners and promoters, customers declined to come. Chicago had been a new, bursting-at-the-scenes city on the rise. Not only was the exposition a big draw, but the whole of the Midwest looked to Chicago as the likeliest place to find entertainment. So in they flowed.

The same could not be said for south Brooklyn. New Yorkers, then as now, always have too much entertainment to choose from. Cody was no longer a novelty and there were troupes of many sorts to lure the crowds.

The failure was sharp and painful. Within six months of his greatest financial triumph Cody was forced to borrow $5,000 from Salsbury. In south Brooklyn it cost nearly that much a day just to feed the performers and mount the show.

To make matters worse, it was just at this troubled point that Nate Salsbury's health began to fail. Cody himself was occasionally under the weather, probably because he was drinking heavily again.

But the big troupe of riders and performers had been laboriously acquired and neither of the half-sick showmen wanted to let them go. A few performers peeled off and went to Pawnee Bill but most stayed put and tucked in their three meals a day while the bosses did some serious thinking.

The thinking soon yielded a solution that promised profits: they hired the mostly unsung junior partner of P. T. Barnum, the man who, more than any other, had mastered the logistics of moving large companies of performers around America in the cheapest and most efficient way.

His name was James Bailey. South Brooklyn was soon abandoned and Buffalo Bill's Wild West, grown yet larger by the addition of some colorful Zouaves, set out on the road. Annie Oakley and Frank Butler had their own railroad car, one of the eighty-two that it took to transport this vast company from place to place. At one point the Wild West performed in as many as 130 towns a year, many of them so small that they had never expected anything as exciting as Buffalo Bill's Wild West to show up in their neighborhood. Bailey added sideshows, making the Wild West more circuslike. At one point Salsbury, not content, decided that minstrel shows were the coming thing; he soon had three hundred black performers going from town to town across the South. But the black Wild West did not succeed.

11

WHAT might be called saturation touring became the pattern for Buffalo Bill's Wild West as the nineteenth century moved toward its close. James Bailey knew his business well. He seemed to have a map of the nation's rail system in his head, and an up-to-date timetable as well. He had thoroughly mastered the complex economics of touring companies and kept the show profitable, though with only a minuscule margin of error. Cody and Annie Oakley remained the headliners, becoming, with such broad exposure, even greater superstars than they had been. Johnny Baker's star was also rising.

However, as any touring actor or musician knows, touring takes its toll. Annie and Frank adapted to it better than Cody, whose tendency to burn the candle at both ends left him often irritable.

When the Spanish-American War broke out in 1898, Cody, who had been running his Congress of Rough Riders for some years, was naturally expected to volunteer. How could America have a war without Buffalo Bill? His old friend General Miles, who seemed to turn to Cody in every military emergency, naturally urged him to take a command. Cody was probably in no mood for war at this time, but he grandly offered to provide forty-five scouts and four hundred horses, though his troupe owned only about 450 at this time. Nothing more was heard of this offer—Buffalo Bill did not fight in the Spanish-American War. Theodore Roosevelt soon recruited his own Rough Riders; it is unlikely that T.R. would have wanted to share the stage with Cody anyway. General Miles himself made only a modest contribution to the conflict, just as it was winding down.

The Wild West continued to tour, always running just a step or two ahead of financial disaster. Don Russell pointed out that Cody was trapped by his own ambition. He couldn't afford either to quit or not to quit. He was still making good money, so much that he couldn't afford to turn it down, and yet, if he had stopped touring, he would have been broke within two months.

12

WHEN the nineteenth century ended William F. Cody was undoubtedly one of the most famous people on earth. Most of the seventeen hundred dime novels that featured him had already been published. Tens of thousands of photographs of him had been taken; tens of thousands of posters showing him on a horse had been distributed. James Bailey had concluded that 130 shows a year might be pushing it, but the Wild West still did at least one hundred, and the troupe still employed nearly five hundred people. Virtually every celebrity to pass through America since 1883 had seen at least one performance, including Sarah Bernhardt. Cody had met every president and was an icon looked up to by millions of American children.

Cody was only fifty-four when the century ended—they had been very active years but he had not lost his looks and, for that matter, never would. Nobody in America looked better on a horse, an asset he exploited until the end of his life, in 1917. He was an unusually buoyant, optimistic man. Had he been a worrier he might well have worried himself into the grave years earlier, but despite myriad troubles he had the ability to relax and recharge. In show business he had, essentially, no way to go but down; the same comment could be made for almost anyone of a certain age in show business; and yet, as he partnered with various people and plunged into venture after venture, he frequently managed to rise again, to find pockets of profitability that no one else could have found.

There is no doubt, though, that for the last fifteen years of his life he was in a long footrace with his creditors. The footrace, from time to time, left him feeling very worn out. Various of his competitors were always counting him out, only to have him bob up again. As late as 1905, after Annie Oakley had left the show, Cody had one of his most profitable runs ever, in Paris. A year later, in Marseilles, he had such a spectacular opening week that he decided he could afford to donate $5,000 to victims of the eruption of Mount Vesuvius; but these bright moments were soon shadowed by the death of James Bailey, who had so brilliantly managed the enterprise for some twelve years. Salsbury had died in 1902. The 1907 season was the first ever in which Buffalo Bill Cody was sole manager of his own show. From its incorporation in 1883 either Nate Salsbury or James Bailey had done most of the organizational work.

But a big show was planned for Madison Square Garden and there was no one to run it but Cody himself. Many expected him to falter, or throw up his hands, but he didn't, nor did he during the next two years of touring. According to his own testimony he was in his office by eight-thirty every morning and he worked all day, though, as he frankly admitted, such desk work was not his forte.

By this point Cody only owned one-third of his own show. The Bailey estate had bought out Salsbury's interest; they owned two-thirds. A $13,000 note turned up in the Bailey documents. Cody said he had paid it but the Baileys weren't so sure. Cody certainly did his best to manage the show well and protect the Baileys' interest. The $13,000 note is worth mentioning only because squabbles over credit were to be a feature of the rest of Cody's life.

Cody had carried on a fairly polite rivalry with Gordon Lillie (Pawnee Bill) for many years. Cody irritated Lillie by lording it over him, but eventually it became clear to both men that they ought to team up, so Buffalo Bill's Wild West with Pawnee Bill's Wild East did good business for a while. The Wild East featured musical elephants, camel caravans, boomerang throwers, fakirs, and the like. When Annie Oakley considered coming out of retirement in 1909, Cody and Lillie tried to hire her, but she went instead with a new show, called Young Buffalo's Wild West, for a few years, and then left show business again.

Eventually Gordon Lillie bought out the Baileys' two-thirds interest in the Wild West. He had already acquired Cody's third. Finally, as sole owner of the world's most famous troupe, Lillie got to lord it over Cody a bit. He was usually generous with Cody—for one thing he saw to the cancellation of the $13,000 note; this was part of his deal with the Baileys. Buffalo Bill and Pawnee Bill could neither live with nor live without one another—wranglings over who owed how much to whom continued until the end of Cody's life.

13

L ATE in October 1901, Buffalo Bill's Wild West was traveling
deep into the night, bound for Danville, Virginia, where they
would play their last engagement of the year. All the performers were
probably looking forward to being home, if they had homes apart
from the show itself. Annie Oakley and Frank Butler were asleep in
their private car.

At three in the morning a railroad engineer named Lynch, perhaps not realizing that the show train consisted of two sections,
pulled a switch at the wrong time, so that the show train plowed into
a freight train loaded with fertilizer. Brakemen on both trains realized that calamity was inevitable but managed to slow the trains to a
speed of about eight miles an hour when they collided.

Even so the carnage was horrifying, with the cars carrying
livestock being the worst hit. Five cars full of horses were almost
wholly lost; hundreds of horses either died outright or had to be
killed. Cody and Johnny Baker estimated the loss as between
$50,000 and $60,000—a worse calamity even than the sinking of the
steamboat.

Fortunately the show's personnel were traveling in the rear
cars—no employee was much more than shaken up by the collision.
Frank Butler told reporters that his watch got smashed—Annie Oakley had wrenched her back. Both Butlers walked away from the
wreck readily enough—news stories focused on the loss of the horses
and other livestock.

The fact is, however, that Annie Oakley never fired another shot as a member of Buffalo Bill's Wild West. She retired, and maintained that her retirement was necessary because of the dreadful internal injuries that she suffered in the train wreck. Frank Butler, who at the time said everything was fine, later maintained that his wife had sustained a terrible injury to her hip.

Most of the early biographers, including the usually hard to fool Walter Havighurst, accepted the "dreadful injury" theory of Annie's retirement; but recently Shirl Kasper has given all this the lie. Less than two months after the wreck, Kasper points out, Annie competed in a shoot near Lake Denmark, New Jersey, and hit twenty-three of twenty-five live pigeons. A reporter for *American Field* praised her shooting highly and mentions that she was quite recovered from the shaking up she had received in the train wreck. Not only did she appear to be in her usual good health, but her long hair was evidently still lustrous and brown, as it had been during all her years as a performer. Had it mysteriously changed color, as women's hair sometimes does, someone at this well-attended shoot would no doubt have commented on the change.

The competition at Lake Denmark occurred on the seventeenth of December 1901. Only a month later, the sixteenth of January 1902, Annie competed at another shoot, this one on Long Island. She shot well and appeared to be in fine health, but except for a strand here and there, her hair had turned snow white.

What happened?

Frank Butler, who lost nothing but a watch in the train wreck, maintained that the shock of the collision was so great that his wife's hair had, within about eighteen hours, turned white. It hadn't, of course, or someone would have noticed it at Lake Denmark, or even sooner, given the publicity the big train wreck received.

Shirl Kasper's dogged sleuthing turned up two clippings in a scrapbook Annie Oakley kept, both blaming the hair color change on an inattentive attendant at a spa in Arkansas, very likely the famous Hot Springs, which Annie liked and often visited. She was left too long in a bath too hot and her hair turned. It may be that Annie gave this explanation to a friend, never supposing it would surface in a newspaper. Kasper thinks that Annie's obsessive modesty made her

reluctant to admit that she had been scantily clad, even for thera-
peutic purposes.

As to leaving the show, perhaps she was merely tired of touring.
She may have been emboldened to retire because Frank had just secured a lucrative job as the representative of an ammunition company. The Butlers no doubt felt that Frank's new salary, plus what
Annie could earn in shooting competitions, would keep them
nicely—and it did.

It is perhaps worth mentioning that Frank Butler's job with the
cartridge company relied on what is now called product placement—
the conspicuous use of brand-name products in shows and exhibitions was going strong in Cody's day. Buffalo Bill was advertised as
using only Winchester ammunition. Annie Oakley only shot Stevens
shotguns, while Johnny Baker had an exclusive commitment to the
Parker arms company.

In 1903, a couple of years after Annie's hair turned white, an incident
occurred that shocked her so that her hair might well have turned
white had it not already been white. A story appeared in Hearst's
Chicago papers, the *Examiner* and the *American*, with this headline:

ANNIE OAKLEY ASKS COURT FOR MERCY!

The reporter, somewhat incredibly even for Hearst, informed the
public that Annie Oakley was in jail for stealing the trousers of a
black man, meaning to sell them and buy cocaine. Given Annie's extreme modesty, the notion that she would touch the trousers of any
man except her husband, and then only to launder them, must have
sent her reeling. The story, written by a reporter named Ernest Stout,
went out over the Publishers Press wire and was picked up by many
newspapers all over the country. Astonished friends, who knew the
story couldn't be true, clipped the stories and sent them to Nutley,
New Jersey, where the Butlers were then living. The more Annie
read, the angrier she became.

The fact that the story could be easily disproved didn't really as-
suage the hurt and fury. It was easy enough to establish that she had

not been in Chicago for more than a year, but what may have hurt most in the absurd story was the suggestion that she was poor. In her youth she *had* been poor—she knew its terrors and shame too well.

That Hearst ran this story, which he knew would be picked up by many newspapers, suggests how uncritical the world of yellow journalism really was. It was tabloid journalism, pitched well beyond the boundaries of believability. Nowadays such a story might claim that Hillary Clinton had sex with aliens, or something of the sort. Nonetheless, the effect on Annie Oakley was real.

For the next five years Annie went about the tiresome, expensive business of clearing her name. Her whole life had been devoted to building her reputation as a lady, and a lady of firm character as well. She was not about to see it lost. The libel process was tricky, as it is now, but she pursued her nemesis with the same determination that she had once applied to her shooting.

According to Shirl Kasper, the first twenty newspapers she sued paid her sizable libel fees. Hearst, in an effort to sully her if he could, sent a reporter to Greenville, where the Butlers had moved; but the locals were so outraged that someone was trying to dig up dirt on their beloved Annie that the town refused the detective a room for the night.

When the trials began, Annie was often sharp-spoken in her own defense. She denied having ever turned somersaults in her act; she denied having worn leggings, or having allowed her skirts to fall. When asked about education she said it was a very good thing in a person with common sense but a very bad thing in the hands of a cheap lawyer.

In time she sued fifty-five newspapers, collecting from all but one. Many of the awards were merely tokens but Hearst had to cough up $27,000 at least. Frank Butler claimed that every cent earned above their legal expenses went to charity, but that may not have been strictly true. The Butlers didn't live lavishly—Annie was too frugal for that—but they did live well.

Competitive shooting remained a very popular sport. In 1916 the *New York Times* claimed that 36 million clay pigeons had been broken in that one year alone. Annie Oakley—although she chose her shoots carefully—probably broke several thousand of that total.

She still, though, encountered the occasional snub from patrons of the all-male clubs. She was thus very pleased when, in 1913, a rich woman in Wilmington, Delaware, opened the first shooting club for women only.

Frank began to tour a little with his company's shooting team; sometimes Annie went with him. In a big shoot in Kansas City in 1902 she encountered her old rival, Lillian Smith, who had since been adopted into the Sioux tribe, shooting under the name of Wenona. Essentially, Lillian was in vaudeville. Whether the two met, or what they had to say to one another, is not recorded.

The elite trapshooting circles in those days attracted wealthy men who were usually very good shots. Someone not wealthy would not have been able to afford the travel, or the ammunition. For much of his life Frank Butler shot as well as his wife—he won his share of competitions—but he accepted the fact that Annie was the star; living in her shadow did not seem to bother him. Annie may have had a little more grit and a little more stamina. In 1906 she hit 1,016 brass discs without a miss. She was competitive, she enjoyed winning, and to the end, she was reluctant to pass up money.

14

WHY, when she decided to return to touring in 1911, Annie chose the fledgling Young Buffalo's Wild West, is something of a mystery. She did visit Cody and Gordon Lillie first; she had worked for both of them and liked them. Perhaps she merely wanted a higher salary than that beleaguered pair could readily afford. Perhaps the maintenance upkeep on a major star was more than they felt they could undertake. Annie may have had no desire to upstage Johnny Baker, who was the big shooting attraction at the time. Perhaps she liked it that Young Buffalo's show was a little more circus-like, with six elephants and some very talented clowns.

When she quit Young Buffalo in 1913 she was through with touring forever, though not entirely through with show business. The movies were beckoning. She had been persuaded to take a primitive screen test, though not much came of overtures from this new medium. She was fifty-three at the time. A little later she had her last encounter with Cody, an old man by then and already sadly in the grip of the financier Harry Tammen. Cody and Gordon Lillie had been operating a kind of half circus called the Two Bills Show. Although Cody only owned half the show he unwisely made a note to Tammen that failed to secure Lillie's half for Lillie. When the note came due Tammen sold the livestock and equipment at a sheriff's auction. Though Gordon Lillie was financially well off, he probably—and with justice—never forgave Cody for this last betrayal. Cody may not have forgiven himself either—he knew that what he had done was disgraceful, but by then he was leading a slipping-down life and could not arrest the slippage.

15

OVER the years, whenever Cody fancied himself somewhat ahead in the financial game, he formed the habit of sending sizable sums of money home to Lulu, back in North Platte, with the instruction to buy real estate. Lulu had always been nothing if not practical. She was well capable of securing a good piece of land, or a well-constructed house, if one came on the market.

Cody, of course, thought he was building himself a secure financial position by this method. If the show failed he always had his holdings in North Platte. He could ranch if necessary. He could sell some of that cheaply acquired property.

Imagine his shock, when he found himself in a financial crisis in the 1880s, to discover that this financial haven did not exist. Lulu had been buying real estate all right, and buying it as shrewdly as he had expected, but the catch was that she had put every plank and acre in her own name. Except for his interest in Scout's Rest, where Lulu would no longer consent to live, he owned nothing much in Nebraska that could be turned into ready cash. The cushion he had been counting on simply did not exist.

No doubt Cody laid heavy siege to Lulu at this time—after all, she was still his wife. He knew he hadn't been a perfect husband, but neither had he been a total scoundrel—at least not in his opinion. Hadn't he provided for her handsomely? Hadn't he left her more or less unrestricted?

In Lulu's mind he had left her far too unrestricted—in her mind that meant loneliness and abandonment. She quarreled frequently with his sisters—she thought brother Bill was far too generous with them.

Nor could she reconcile herself to his girlfriends. This came out in court depositions in 1905, when Cody was trying to divorce her. Not only was Lulu jealous of Queen Victoria and Princess Alexandra, there were other less distant women to provoke her jealousies, the actress Katherine Clemmons being one. But there were a number of others, and when Lulu's temper was up, the mere mention of any of them was enough to put her into a glass-breaking mood. At one point, hearing a female voice in her husband's room in New York, she proceeded to destroy her own well-appointed room. This fit, which must have been spectacular, cost Cody more than $300.

Though the Cody marriage constantly veered from melodrama to farce, there were elements in it which were genuinely heartbreaking. Lulu had married for love, but her husband moved her to an ugly prairie town and left her. She spent much of her life feeling abandoned. Cody was never any particular help with the children. He provided well financially—Lulu was never impoverished—but he didn't provide well emotionally. Clearly Lulu would rather have had less money and more time with Bill—that is, she would have until she grew hardened.

Cody never entirely lost his affection for his wife—it was just that his affection was fitful. He made one of his brothers-in-law, Al Goodman, general manager of the Nebraska properties, with instructions to try not to mind Lulu. Here, from a letter he wrote Goodman: "I often feel very sorry for her. She is a strange woman, but don't mind her—remember she is my wife—and let it go at that. If she gets cranky just laugh at it, she can't help it."

But the kettle of the Cody marriage continued to seethe, seething and seething for more than forty years. Cody's actress-kissing tendencies were always likely to surface. At one point Lulu strongly suspected that he had bestowed a kiss or two on his press agent, Bessie Isbell, after her visit to North Platte.

An odd, sad grievance surfaced in the divorce proceedings in 1905. One of the reasons he wanted out, Cody claimed, was that Lulu had tried to poison him on a Christmas visit in 1900. The artist Dan Muller was witness to this strange incident and confirms that

Cody collapsed and was temporarily deprived of speech, while having some sort of drink with his wife. Dan Muller loved Lulu, and knew she was not a poisoner, but something had happened to bring the Colonel low that night.

The "something" turned out to be a love potion that Lulu, in her desperation, had purchased from a Gypsy. It was called Dragon's Blood. What it contained nobody knows, but its purpose, of course, was to enable Lulu to recapture Bill Cody's affections. After thirty years, she was still trying.

Lulu's attorney suggested that it was probably not the first time that Colonel Cody had been falling-down drunk—but the fact of the Dragon's Blood was soon revealed.

16

DESPITE his looks, fame, and willingness to kiss girls, Buffalo Bill Cody was not a notable success with women. The first one, after Lulu, to bedevil him was the American actress Katherine Clemmons, whom Cody met during his first London show. She was good-looking, but no Bernhardt or Duse, as Cody fondly supposed her to be. He financed one play in England and another in America, the latter a spectacular flop that cost Cody many thousands.

Katherine Clemmons was an energetic opportunist. She had had a frontier background and was more than able to keep up with Cody when it came to drinking. How much she ever cared for Bill Cody is at this distance hard to say, but he was far from being the only suitor to enjoy her favors. She was tempestuous and could match Lulu fit for fit if need be. Perhaps the fits were what prompted Cody to say that he had rather manage a million Indians than one soubrette.

Still, the two carried on for a few years, until Katherine Clemmons concluded, accurately, that Cody didn't really have much money and would be more than likely to lose most of what he had. She was looking for bigger bucks and secured them—or supposed she had—by marrying the son of the fabulously wealthy Jay Gould. Howard Gould was as eligible a bachelor as anyone could hope for, but by 1907 he divorced Katherine, citing infidelity with several men, one of them Buffalo Bill Cody.

The end of this sordid story does Cody great credit. During the divorce proceedings the Goulds offered Cody a goodly sum—$50,000—if he would testify against Katherine. Cody, though desperate for money at the time, threw the gentlemen out of the room.

Lulu wasn't always on the attack. During the divorce proceedings, which failed, she remarked to one reporter that "Will was the kindest and most generous of men."

Cody proved to be a terrible witness for himself. Aside from the ridiculous matter of the poisoning he couldn't come up with any convincing reason as to why the judge should grant him a divorce. He could not remember dates or incidents, and was constantly tripped up in his testimony, not only by Lulu's lawyers but by his own.

Divorce was no snap in 1905. The judge believed every word Lulu uttered, but believed few words of Cody's. He rejected the petition, leaving the Codys to struggle on with one another for another dozen years.

17

EXCEPT for his misguided attempt to ride the brute buffalo known as Monarch, Buffalo Bill, as a showman, did well with his namesake animal, the buffalo. Horses were another matter. He lost nearly five hundred in the big train wreck near Danville in 1901, and disaster was to strike his horse herd a second time, in Europe in 1906, when the show horses were stricken with glanders, reducing their numbers by two-thirds.

Cody's was hardly the only touring company to find itself at the mercy of events. The Miller Brothers' famous 101 Ranch troupe toured with some success in the years before World War I—the Millers sported the amazing black bulldogger Bill Pickett. Will Rogers sometimes practiced his rope tricks at the 101 Ranch, and movie star Tom Mix had worked there as a cowboy.

Nonetheless it fell to the Millers to launch the worst-timed Wild West tour of all time: they set out to play Europe in the early fall of 1914. Not long before sailing for England one of the Millers had purchased a lot of half-broken Mexican horses, figuring to tame them as they went along, but they had scarcely disembarked in London when their entire herd was requisitioned for the British war effort. A lot of these unruly Mexican steeds soon saw service on the Western front—very likely most of them were eaten. This tour, or rather nontour, became a nightmare for the Millers. They had already loaned out some Indians to a German circus before the guns began to roar. Getting these Indians back to the States was not easy, but most finally managed to return through Scandinavia.

Cody's reputation as a lackadaisical figurehead who left all administrative work to Salsbury or Bailey was a little unfair. He was always prone to jaunts—the freedom to enjoy the Western plains and mountains never lost its appeal to Cody. A jaunt or a hunting trip rarely failed to restore his spirits. One of Katherine Clemmons's big issues with Cody was his tendency to leave on short notice, or no notice. If a bear hunt was offered just as one of Katherine's ponderous plays was opening, Cody more often than not chose the bear hunt.

He could, though, work when he had to. Not long after Nate Salsbury's death he penned this complaint:

> . . . with the death of my partner I have all the more to
> do . . . & more responsibility . . . every day, year in and
> year out, is a rush day for me. I cannot even get one hour
> to myself to quiet my nerves. Someone wants my time all
> the time. I have to attend to my own business—and re-
> ceive company at the same time—to say nothing of the let-
> ters I am compelled to write.

It was plain that a company employing over five hundred people and at least that many animals could not be run from a Western campfire, between attempts to locate bears. Cody grew up on the plains; half his life had been spent under the great skies of the West. Yet for most of the second half of his life he was an urban man, a traveler amid the capitals of Europe. Doubtless he enjoyed many of his urban possibilities—actresses, for example; but undoubtedly there were times when he would have liked to chuck it all and go back to North Platte, a choice now rendered impossible because of Lulu's stubborn refusal to allow him any access to the money she had saved.

In fact, Cody was never—financially—in a position to chuck it all. Despite his endless financial crises and defeats, he remained eternally optimistic about the future. Many propositions came his way: mining ventures, hotels in scenic spots, irrigation schemes to make the desert flower, and of course, inventions and patent medicines on the order of White Beaver's Laugh Cream.

Cody may have made a little money here and there—he invested in so many schemes that one or two of them probably paid off—but the bottom line, always, was that his main asset was himself. People would come in sizable numbers just to see him ride his horse and shoot glass balls. It was as a showman, showing mainly himself, that Cody got the money to pay his bills. Sometimes he even got a little ahead.

The administrative skill that it took to organize large touring companies is uncommon in any time; Cody was lucky to find, first, Salsbury and then Bailey. Salsbury, observing James Bailey while he still worked with Barnum, left a short description of that well-known modern figure, the workaholic:

> Bailey's capacity for work is enormous, or at least it seems so to me, for I never hear of him devoting any time to anything but work. He told me himself that he cared for nothing but to make a success of his business at any cost. I never heard of him taking any sort of social pleasure. I do not believe he ever attended a theatre or any other form of amusement for the sake of the amusement.

But Salsbury only lasted until 1902, and Bailey to 1906, after which the crème de la crème of big-show managers were no longer available, which is why Bill Cody hitched up his belt and sat down at his desk every morning at eight-thirty. But as he said, desk work was not his forte; and it was the clear need for administrative help, as well as solid financing, that caused him to turn in 1908 to his old rival Gordon Lillie, or Pawnee Bill.

Lillie and Cody had known one another a long time. Cody was fifteen years older than Lillie; the latter was at first, and in some way remained, a good deal starstruck. Lillie had taught for a while at the Pawnee agency; he served as interpreter when Cody and Doc Carver were trying to recruit a few Pawnees for their first show. Lillie was there the day Monarch put Cody in the hospital. Cody may have lorded it over the younger man too much, and he certainly was wrong to blithely imperil Lillie's half of the Two Bills show, but through it all, Lillie remained clear about one thing: Buffalo Bill was still the biggest name, and the most solid asset, in the touring world of that time. If you had Buffalo Bill, the seats would not be empty. It was because of this certainty that Lillie persuaded the Bailey family to forgive the $13,000 note. He wanted to give Buffalo Bill's Wild West with Pawnee Bill's Wild East a chance. (What to us seem cumbersome titles did not discourage the crowds of the time. When Bill Cody worked briefly for the Miller Brothers the show was called "The Military Preparedness, Buffalo Bill [Himself] Combined with the 101 Ranch Show." The show was a combination rodeo and military review, and didn't last long.)

Pawnee Bill took a natural, if short-lived, satisfaction in finally becoming the boss of his old hero. He tolerated Cody's weaknesses and kept things on a fairly even keel.

When Cody died Lillie was deeply moved. "I was a friend of Buffalo Bill's until he died," he said. "He was just an irresponsible boy."

Many would have agreed with Gordon Lillie, but most would have agreed, too, that Cody's irresponsibility wasn't the whole story.

18

BEFORE Buffalo Bill and Gordon Lillie finally split, they took one more big step in unison: they made a movie together. Neither feared innovation and both saw that moving pictures were the coming thing. Cody had started lighting his arenas with Edison's electric lights as early as 1893. He was always buying generators and dynamos, hanging more lights, acquiring the latest gadgets. Several pioneering cameramen filmed scenes from the Wild West shows. Cody was caught by the kinetoscope many times as he made his grand entry. There were movie booths in the St. Louis Exposition of 1904—the first of many movies about Cody's idol Kit Carson appeared in that year.

By the turn of the century cameramen were ubiquitous. Annie Oakley was screen-tested more than once; there may still exist somewhere a few faded frames of her performing at shooting contests, breaking clay pigeon after clay pigeon. We have fairly full reports of the making of many films in the first decade of the twentieth century, but precious little of this early footage survives.

Cody had survived as a showman since 1872 by repeating, over and over in simple skits, the story of the Plains Indian wars. He saw no reason not to continue repeating it in this new and potentially thrilling medium—neither did Pawnee Bill. And where better to begin than with the story of Cody's life. *The Life of Buffalo Bill* was a one-reeler filmed in 1912 by the Buffalo Bill and Pawnee Bill film company.

In the opening sequence Cody plays himself, an old scout making a lonely camp on a lonely trail. The old scout has a dream in which an actor playing Cody relives Cody's much-relived life. Indians dash about, chasing stagecoaches; then, as the centerpiece to a well-planned dream, there's the duel with Yellow Hair. The story, as well as the characters, move at a furious pace.

The partners were proud of this maiden work, but by 1912 they were by no means the only showmen around who were making Westerns. According to Joy Kasson, Biograph, by 1912, had already made seventy Westerns, some of them directed by D. W. Griffith. One of the most famous of these was the Mary Pickford version of *Ramona*.

Pawnee Bill seemed to find filmmaking even messier and more chaotic than putting on arena shows; he was not wrong. The strain soon wore him down; he retired to his ranch in the far West and lived until 1942.

Cody, however, saw a chance to do something really ambitious, something that could preserve for future generations of Americans the grand story of the settling of the West. It might also, if it worked, restore both his fortunes and his self-respect.

What he proposed, and mostly completed, was a work called *Indian War Pictures* (though, at various times, this sequence of films used many more titles, *Buffalo Bill's War Pictures* being one of the more ordinary). This was not to be one film but several, which would, of course, touch many of the old bases: Killing of Tall Bull, First Scalp for Custer, and so forth. Cody managed to get his old friend General Miles interested—movies were such a big attraction in those years that a man of Cody's fame had not too much difficulty in securing financing. Before he was through he even secured some from Harry Tammen, although he surely knew by this time how unscrupulous Tammen was.

When Cody set out to restore his name by making motion pictures, he decided that their hallmark would be authenticity, an elusive element in any art at any time. He always tried to make his arena shows as realistic as possible by using real props (the Deadwood stage) and, in many cases, real Westerners such as John Y. Nelson and, of course, the many Indians. Cody managed, throughout his long career, to think of himself as mainly a kind of pictorial historian. He tried, to the best of his abilities, to show Western life as it had been. And he also managed to sustain a forty-year career playing only one character, himself.

Some of the old tropes from his arena shows worked fairly well as short films. The Battle of Summit Springs (Tall Bull) and the First Scalp for Custer (Yellow Hair) presented no huge problems to the filmmakers—after all, only a couple of years later D. W. Griffith would mass thousands of extras for his great film *Intolerance*. There were people of experience who could direct Westerns competently. Joy Kasson's estimate is that Westerns comprised about twenty percent of American film production by then. The early Western star Bronco Billy (Anderson) had already made some 150.

At first things went swimmingly for *Indian War Pictures*, but Cody had never been good at quitting while he was ahead. In this instance his miscalculation was his decision to finish the Indian Wars sequence with a reenactment of Wounded Knee, the horror that had taken place only twenty-three years earlier.

Cody had been blocked from visiting Sitting Bull before he was killed, and had not himself witnessed the carnage on the battlefield. Black Elk had not yet made his famous statement about the broken hoop, the sacred tree, and the death of his people's dream. What Cody failed to realize was that, for the Sioux people, Wounded Knee was a scar that had not healed and would never heal. They were not ready to go back to that place where so many warriors, women, and children had died. Though they knew the difference between real life and playacting—Cody himself had employed many of them—they may not have believed that General Miles and his six hundred soldiers were arriving just to make a show.

Perhaps the guns were loaded with blanks, but not every Sioux was convinced of that. The Sioux women in particular were very disturbed; some, it is reported, began to sing their death songs.

Cody had not reckoned with the swelling up of pain and anger that this particular reenactment produced, not all of it on the Indians' side. There was a rift between Cody and Miles, because the latter insisted that the eleven thousand soldiers that had assembled at Pine

Ridge to accept the Sioux surrender on January 16, 1890, be faithfully represented.

Cody was for authenticity, but not authenticity on quite such an expensive scale. So the six hundred soldiers had to be marched around and around in front of the cameras. Though General Miles didn't know it, most of the cameras contained no film.

The shoot at Wounded Knee took thirty-four days in the fall of 1913 and produced some thirty thousand feet of film. It was released in various formats (five, six, and eight reels), all of which failed. It appeared under a variety of titles, but changing the title didn't help. Both Tammen and the ever-loyal John Burke tried to promote it but nothing worked. Cody even rode his famous horse Isham onstage in Denver. He got a cheer, of course, but that did nothing for the show in Chicago. Cody's reputation didn't suffer from this failure, but his fortune was not recouped.

The negative for this film is lost, and the copy in the Cody museum has deteriorated beyond repair. Nothing now remains of Cody's ambitious effort except a few faded fragments and a set of remarkable still photos, which show Cody, gaunt and old now, scalping Yellow Hair yet one more time. A version called *The Adventures of Buffalo Bill*, released in 1917 to take advantage of Cody's death, also failed.

In trying to redo the massacre of Wounded Knee, Cody had taken matters too far, and pleased no one. The military hated the picture because it made them look like the killers they had been. The public avoided it because it slammed home the uncomfortable fact that the destruction of the Indians and their tribal lifeways had been a brutal tragedy.

What Cody felt is hard to know. He knew that he had spent much of his life recycling his own early experience—he was now an old man. The way of life he had loved best, the scout's free life in the good air of the West, was as gone now as the buffalo that had helped make his fame. The West was settled, the frontier was closed. Most of the friends of his youth—Texas Jack Omohundro, Wild Bill Hickok—were dead. His most ambitious effort to show what it had been like in the old West—the *Indian War Pictures*—had failed in part *because* of its authenticity. He had spent much of his life peddling illusions about the West and the illusions succeeded where the reality failed. He had been right at the beginning, correctly perceiving that it was illusion that the people wanted. The reality, whether they had lived it or not, just wasn't as appealing.

Reality might not sell, but the man himself, Buffalo Bill, was still wanted, still a great draw. Even as late as 1914 a variety show in London offered him $2,500 a week just to appear; Cody turned them down—he thought he was worth twice as much.

One of the things he fancied might save him was the dude ranch. Had he not just spent forty years watching young Eastern women go nuts over cowboys? Wouldn't well-heeled Easterners pay to spend a month or two on a "ranch" in the West, riding horses, punching cattle in a light way, and singing corny songs around campfires under the great Western sky?

Again, Cody was right. They would pay. It could be argued that the survival of ranching in Montana and Wyoming is the result of the fact that so many Eastern girls came west and married cowboys, bringing their money and their taste with them. Sheridan, Wyoming, where the queen of England comes occasionally to buy racehorses, probably has the best small-town public library in America. Visitors to Sheridan may even be entertained in one of Cody's houses. In that part of the West his influence is still very much felt.

19

ANNIE OAKLEY never lost her great appeal to crowds. Once in a while she performed at big fairs, and the magic was still there. In the main her retirement was pleasant. She and Frank were particularly fond of a resort hotel called the Carolina, in Pinehurst, North Carolina. They stayed there often, enjoying plantation quail shooting, and now and then a duck hunt.

Both Butlers still occasionally competed in shooting matches, but Annie more and more preferred to sponsor shooting clinics, mostly for women. She claimed to have taught some fifteen thousand women how to shoot. When World War I broke out the clinics found it difficult, for a time, to get either revolvers or ammunition. Several times Annie remembered how much she had disliked the Kaiser—after all, millions might not have lost their lives if she had just shot the Kaiser rather than his cigarette.

However comfortable Annie may have been with Frank Butler as a husband—it is doubtful that her eye ever roved—common domesticity was something that had never really suited her. Frank himself, though he doted on Annie, was bold enough to point this out:

> Her shooting record is much better than her housekeeping mark . . . Riding, shooting and dancing come naturally to her but she is a rotten housekeeper . . . her record in this department is seven cooks in five days.

Indeed, Annie admitted to being extremely picky. Details mattered to her. All too often closets were positioned wrong, or sinks would be too high, lights were too bright or else not bright enough. Without the spur of competition to drain off her energies her pickiness was sure to intensify. She did like dancing, though, and once won a prize at the Carolina Hotel at a dance in which she came dressed as an Indian woman, with feathers in her hair.

Despite the comforts of the Carolina Hotel, or of the various nice houses the Butlers occupied for varying lengths of time, the Butlers were more or less rolling stones. Annie readily agreed with her husband that she was not meant for homemaking—she was still in some ways the bohemian wood sprite who liked to go out amid the trees and the critters with her gun.

"You can't cage a Gypsy," she admitted once. "I went all to pieces under the care of a house."

The Butlers kept on the move, but they were leisurely moves— they always took their guns and their dogs, and sometimes their boat. Annie was asked to do many charity shoots and usually accepted. She had been a poor child and her memory was long. She often contributed to poor farms and orphanages. When she toured with Young Buffalo she followed the example set by Cody and Salsbury in Chicago—free tickets went to orphans, particularly the poor orphans of Darke County, Ohio, where she had grown up.

Annie Oakley had traveled the world, shooting and winning. She was a high achiever, as Type A as anyone could be. She felt, and said, that—except for heavy lifting—she was the equal of any man at anything. But she resisted feminism per se and was ambivalent about giving women the vote. Cody was all for suffrage and argued with her about it. Working outside the home and earning a salary seemed better to him than staying home with the cat.

Annie wasn't so sure. She thought she might be for suffrage if only the good women would vote. But she was never particularly indulgent about her sex and worried about what might happen if too many bad women voted.

Part of her objection to feminism seemed to be an aesthetic objection to bloomers. She hated them and, so far as is known, never wore them. In her day all real ladies wore skirts, and that was that. She was, after all, a mainly Victorian lady, although she certainly expanded the bounds of that role when she took up show business.

On the other hand she was adamant in her belief that women deserved to be, and should be, armed. Modesty and fear of abuse played a part in this belief. Whatever happened to her in the two years she was with the "wolves" was not discussed, but she openly considered rape a threat most women should take seriously. She several times made it clear that she would have no qualms about shooting any man who threatened her honor. "If accosted I could easily fire," she insisted. She thought that every school ought to have a rifle range and that both boys and girls should receive adequate instruction about how to use a firearm.

When World War I broke out Annie even toyed with the idea of organizing and leading a women's regiment, even though it might mean relaxing her role on pants for women. She once broached this idea to Theodore Roosevelt, who immediately told her to forget it.

Unable to load up and attack the Hun directly, Annie did the next best thing, which was to visit army camps and inspire the soldiers with her shooting. She later said that her shooting exhibitions in the camps were more inspiring to her than even her best successes with the Wild West shows.

Annie and Frank were at Pinehurst the day the Great War ended—there was a big victory parade and she capped the festivities by giving an impromptu shooting exhibition.

From then until the end of her life she did more and more charity work. Two of her sisters had died of tuberculosis, so she always contributed to efforts to defeat that disease. At one point she melted down her medals and contributed the money to a sanatorium.

In 1922 she did a much-reported shoot on Long Island for wounded soldiers. This seems to have been the last time she attempted her full act, skipping if she hit and pouting if she missed, as it had been in days of yore, with her patented crowd-pleasing little back kick at the end, the same kick that won her so much applause with the Wild West. And as in days of yore, the crowd absolutely loved her. A film clip survives of this high-profile shoot, with a few frames of Annie coming through a door. It may be that her old friend Fred Stone, a prolific moviemaker, was there with his camera, trying to persuade her to go before the cameras in *The Western Girl* or some other suitable melodrama.

Annie was certainly aware by this time that she was indeed a Gypsy—she was never going to settle down. She had told herself, and the world, many times that she was through with show business. These announcements were her version of Buffalo Bill's countless farewell tours. She probably thought she would be done with show business, but in practice being done with it wasn't that easy. She kept trying to quit, perhaps thinking each time that she *would* quit, but in reality she never did quit—not until her health finally failed her. Once a performer, always a performer; and for a performer who had been a very big star, the business was just not that easy to give up. The attention and the need for competition kept bringing Annie Oakley back.

To a reporter who interviewed her just after a shoot at a big fair in Brockton, Massachusetts, she admitted that the rush of celebrity and the hurly-burly of showbiz still had its seductiveness for her. She also frankly pointed out that she had made $700 for twenty minutes' work. She and Frank Butler never lost sight of the financial picture—how else, other than by shooting, could a sixty-two-year-old woman make $700 in less than half an hour?

Very shortly after the lucrative shoot in Brockton, a car wreck—that increasingly common American disaster—interrupted any plans Annie and Frank might have been nursing in regard to a return to the tour. In early November 1922, the Butlers were in Florida vacationing when their car flipped over, pinning Annie underneath it. Frank was uninjured, but Annie suffered both a broken hip and a broken ankle.

Her injuries were not life-threatening, but they of course had an effect on Annie's morale. Though she didn't know it immediately, she would need to wear a brace on one leg for the rest of her life. She was two months in the hospital, receiving thousands of sympathy cards during her stay.

Still, the next spring, she shot at the Philadelphia Phillies training camp, hitting tossed pennies as readily as ever.

She shot, now and then, at various gatherings, though seldom with quite her old enthusiasm. Once or twice she did summon the old spirit; she even once danced a jig despite her brace.

Then, little by little, she finally began to let show business go. By then she took a certain amount of looking after. Frank, though docile enough, could not be bothered with domestic chores, though he did, now and then, cut a pile of firewood for Annie's little stove. Fortunately the Butlers moved to Ohio, to Darke County in fact, where Annie had four nieces who saw that their famous aunt was well looked after.

When the Butlers made their will, Frank left a little something to his first wife, Elizabeth, and their daughter, Kattie. It makes one wonder where these two had been for forty years. Annie was many things, but she was not a sharer. The other ex-wife and the grown child were never mentioned.

The end of Annie Oakley's story I gave at the beginning of this book. She had anemia, and it worsened; Frank Butler was rapidly fading too. The nieces saw that what could be done was done. Frank, in Michigan, was well taken care of.

Then one day the lady undertaker, Louise Stocker, did her duty. Soon Annie went home up North Star way.

Will Rogers, who loved her, sent this comment: "Whenever I think of Annie Oakley I stop and say to myself: it's what you are, not what you are in, that makes you."

The address on his letter was Beverly Hills, California.

20

WILLIAM F. CODY never lost his looks, though he did lose his hair. As early as the nineties Burke and Salsbury convinced him he would have to make do with hairpieces, and he did so for some twenty years. Occasionally he embarrassed himself by lifting his hairpiece when he lifted his hat. These occasions put him out of temper; he was not without vanity. Also he knew that a legend had to behave like a legend. His appearance, to a large extent, was still his meal ticket.

Despite the many vexations that come with aging, Cody remained a remarkably resilient man. He suffered many lows, but he also rose above many humiliations, the worst of which was the failure of the Two Bills show and the subsequent sale of its assets—mainly livestock—at a sheriff's auction in 1913. After this sad event Cody said of Tammen: "He was the man who had my show sold at a sheriff's sale, which broke my heart." It also broke his relationship with Gordon Lillie, who owned half the show. Some friends, feeling sorry for Cody, bought his show horse Isham at the auction and gave him back to Cody.

Gordon Lillie was not slow in realizing that Tammen got Cody on the ropes financially and set a clever trap: what he wanted and what he got was de facto control of Cody, still in Tammen's eye a very valuable asset. The movie stars were coming. Chaplin, Douglas Fairbanks, Mary Pickford, and others would soon achieve a fame that even Cody's couldn't equal. But for a time there was still plenty of money to be made off Buffalo Bill.

Tammen was right—Cody was still world-famous. It was at this time that the big offer came in from the variety show in England. Though Cody rejected the offer, the mere fact that it had been made convinced him that he could make yet another comeback. Tammen still had him working in the Sells-Floto Circus, but what working meant in this context was mainly just that Cody showed up and made a few trips around the arena, sometimes on Isham, sometimes just in a phaeton. He had stopped breaking glass balls on any regular basis, though sometimes he would break a few as a flourish. He seemed spent, he seemed blocked, and yet it was at about this point that he flung himself into moviemaking, even using some of Tammen's money. Movies were clearly there to stay; Tammen, like many another tycoon in the decades to follow, wanted to get in on the show, meet the stars, bask in the glamour. Harry Tammen would soon learn the bitter lesson that many a tycoon has since learned: movies can lose a lot of money; just swallow it up, as a dry lake swallows water. How could a movie about Buffalo Bill and the Indians lose money? he probably asked himself. He soon found out exactly how, which is not to say that his gamble was a bad one going in.

What defeated the *Indian War Pictures* was Cody's desire for authenticity—this was General Miles's desire too, and in fact, the simpler parts of the *Indian War* skits probably *did* work. Custer's defeat, the attack on the settler's cabin, Cody's scalping of Yellow Hair were effective. What sunk them was the attempt to do Wounded Knee, a huge, tragic event where simplification was not possible. Included in the thirty thousand feet of footage were some scenes of the Ghost Dance as well as the death of Sitting Bull; these, taken alone, might have been effective. But marching the six hundred soldiers around and around the empty camera was just silly.

Besides, the newsreel had been born by this time. In 1915 American audiences were transfixed by the sight of a much more deadly, unfictionalized slaughter—the slaughter that was happening day by day on the Western front in World War I.

When *Indian War Pictures* was finally withdrawn from the movie screens, the greatest showman of his time had only a year or two in which to wander in the shadows of old age. He continued to make occasional appearances, and now and then he would get excited about some new scheme—a mine that couldn't possibly fail, a resort that would soon fill up with Eastern nobs—but these notions were feebly pursued because Cody had no money with which to pursue them. He found himself in the same position as another great hero of the West, the explorer John Charles Frémont, who had once himself had millions but was at the end dependent on what his resourceful wife, Jessie Benton Frémont, could earn with her journalism. On the whole Cody held up better than Frémont, who, in the last photographs, looks very, very distinguished but also very, very sad.

As Cody's finances failed, so did his health. Fortunately, as the end approached, he had his sisters. He had always been extremely generous to his sisters, who were all, of course, convinced that Lulu had neglected him terribly—it had actually been the other way around.

But by this time Lulu too was glad to help—wasn't he still her husband? All his family gathered around and tried to buoy him up.

As he was dying Cody apparently said, "Let my show go on!" and efforts were made to see that he got his last wish. The sharpshooter Johnny Baker, griefstricken at the death of the man who had raised him and given him his calling, managed to bring in the Miller Brothers (they had bought most of the livestock at the Two Bills auction) and a few other old performers, many of them veterans of Cody's shows, and worked up one last tour. This was Cody's true farewell tour, which the boss himself had to miss. Some Indians came. They realized that in losing Pahaska they had lost a friend.

But this short tour was mounted in 1917, while World War I, the Great War, still raged. Buffalo Bill's name was on the marquee one last time but it was the wrong year in which to expect people to be interested in Wild West shows. The farewell tour folded in Nebraska, which was fitting, since the first show had been mounted in Omaha.

21

BUFFALO BILL'S death made big headlines. The Cambridge-born poet E. E. Cummings, then twenty-one years old, read the headlines and scribbled a note or two in his journal.

Some years later, pondering his notes and remembering the man who had inspired the headlines, E. E. Cummings, who had by this time decided to pitch his poetical tent in the lower case alphabet, wrote this poem:

Buffalo Bill's
defunct
            who used to
            ride a watersmooth-silver
                            stallion
and break onetwothreefourfive pigeonsjustlikethat
                                            Jesus

he was a handsome man
                    and what i want to know is
how do you like your blueeyed boy
Mister Death

The most recent and most comprehensive edition of E. E. Cummings's *Complete Poems* is more than eleven hundred pages long. The Buffalo Bill poem is the most famous lyric in this long book, though, of course, we still don't know what Mr. Death thought about his blue-eyed boy.

22

NONE of those who knew Cody well were surprised that he was impoverished at the end. Annie Oakley didn't go to his funeral, but she gave several interviews about him, all of which mentioned his generosity. Once, she remembered, Frank Butler, herself, and Cody came out of a stage door in Manhattan to see a ragged group of bums huddled miserably on a freezing night. Cody at once asked the Butlers how much cash they could scrape up. The three of them managed to dig out $25—Cody insisted on giving $23 of it to the men, ordering them to use it to get a meal and a bunk out of the cold. He and the Butlers, left with $2, dined, as Annie put it, "on simple fare." (She herself had developed such a taste for fare that was not simple that she once reportedly bloomed up to 138 pounds. But she soon got it off and was slim again at the end.)

Everyone who knew Cody mentioned that his weakness was that he could never deny assistance—usually financial—to anyone who asked him. This is not the worst failing a man could have. He may have ended up broke, but he also ended up famous and widely, almost universally, beloved. He was so famous that within a few hours of his death both the president of the United States (Woodrow Wilson) and the king of England (George V) had cabled in condolences and regrets.

The boy who grew up half wild in the Salt River Valley had undoubtedly come a long way. He lived long enough into the movie era to see what huge stars the movies could produce. He may have been bemused by the soaring fame of Chaplin, Mary Pickford, the Gish sisters, William S. Hart. Bemused, but probably not seriously envious. They were wonderful players, but in his time, he had been a big player too—indeed, probably the biggest player, the best-known star. William F. Cody was one of the people who have a fair claim to having invented the star system, for better or for worse.

The man who helped him do it, the faithful press agent John M. Burke, outlived his master and idol by only thirteen weeks.

23

I N the dining room of the Onion Creek Grill, a café in my home-town, Archer City, Texas, there is a Cody poster that I sometimes study if I happen to land in the right booth. It's not really an old poster, but it's old enough to have got smoked up a little—there are suggestions of grease along the lower edge. It's one of thousands of Cody artifacts, but it happened to be hanging in the right place to start me thinking about the man.

Though it is not a very large poster, a great deal of potent im-agery has been crammed into it.

In the center of the poster Cody reclines in an oval, his hair long and loose, his manner benign. Behind him stretch the great prairies of the West. Animals—a little indistinct—graze in the far dis-tance. Cody has a rifle but he is not hunting. The drawing is Flax-man-like. Cody looks about himself with a noble gaze—he might be the Zeus of the West.

Surrounding the central oval is a frieze of the usual high spots from Cody's career. There he is driving a stage, riding with the Over-land Mail, trapping beaver. The frieze is complex and runs all the way around the poster. Of course there is the Taking of the First Scalp for Custer—but then there is also the Challenge Buffalo Hunt, the one some biographers even doubt took place. And finally there is General Sheridan, making Cody chief of scouts before all the troops on the parade ground of a fort. It seems unlikely that Sheri-dan would have ordered up such a show for the scout who had already been doing the work anyway; but there it is, lower left.

The poster, with Cody resting Zeuslike at the center, is emblematic; it attempts to encompass the whole destiny of the American frontier where Cody had lived and acted. Nothing very significant to the long effort of settlement has been left out. There are Indians, plains, buffalo, hunters, soldiers, settlers, even beaver. To my mind the beaver is a particularly important touch. Cody himself trapped beaver for only a few weeks, but beaver provided the first wealth to come out of the West, and they belong in the story. It was the beaver who brought the mountain men, the mountain men who brought the settlers; then the Indians fought the settlers and the soldiers came to fight the Indians. Buffalo Bill, in the frieze, is punching cattle, driving a stagecoach, riding on the Pony Express, scouting for General Sheridan and being honored for it, after which he gets to the right place at the right time and takes the first scalp for Custer.

When it came to cramming the history of the settling of the American West onto one poster, Buffalo Bill Cody knew exactly what to do.

24

S UPERSTARS cannot exactly create themselves, no matter how
skilled—the public can be manipulated vis-à-vis superstars only
up to a point. The public must, at some point, develop a genuine love
for the performer—a love that grows and grows as long as the performer lasts. When great stars die, thousands mourn and mourn
genuinely. Exactly how this chemistry works no one quite under-
stands—but some deep identification is made or superstardom
doesn't happen.

Examples abound. Robert Duvall is a brilliant actor, one of the
finest of his generation. He's never short of work, but he's not a superstar.

As an actor John Wayne was not really in Duvall's class, but as a
performer he was in a higher class: the class of superstars. Why John
Wayne and not Robert Duvall? Who knows? John Ford, who, with
Howard Hawks, made John Wayne a superstar, is supposed to have
said, "The son of a bitch just looks like a man." Wayne, of course,
was a competent but seldom an inspired actor; his famous, slightly
tilted walk was endlessly rehearsed. Was it the walk that made him a
superstar? Or was it something closer to what made Cody a superstar: the sense that this guy just belongs in the West. From *Stagecoach* on Wayne was, in a way, the new Buffalo Bill.

Cody rehearsed his moves too, just as Annie Oakley rehearsed
her shooting tricks and her mannerisms. Without Cody to showcase
her Annie Oakley might have been a celebrated shot, but she would

not likely have become the international star that she became.

And yet, the prominence of Cody's venues doesn't explain her superstardom, either. Perhaps what won the crowd was the little pout when she missed, or her jaunty little back kick when she was pleased—of such tiny but well-rehearsed bits of business are great superstars made. Think of Chaplin—think of Jackie Gleason.

Annie Oakley's stardom was real, just as was Bill Cody's. People liked to see Cody ride his horse fast and pop a few glass balls. He wanted to embody history—the history he had been a part of—and to an extent he did. In this matter he and his audiences were one in that, somehow, they wanted the West, the gloriously dangerous West, the mythic romantic West, the cowboy-and-Indian-filled West, and Cody came closer to giving it to them than anyone else because he had it in *himself* and audiences could see that. He invented rodeo, sponsored cowboys, supported and promoted Indians, many Indians. He drew forth those seventeen hundred dime novels. Thanks to his shows millions of people came to know, or to think they knew, at least a little of what westering, in the broadest sense, had been like.

Whatever his flaws, and there were many, Cody's life work was no mean achievement.

Let Annie Oakley, his greatest star, speaking elegiacally, in terms appropriate to the times, speak the final words:

Goodbye, old friend. The sun setting over the mountain will pay its tribute to the resting place of the last of the great builders of the West, all of which you loved, and part of which you are.

Western Heroes, Heroines, and Villains

HOW LONG THEY LASTED

Meriwether Lewis	1809
Sacagawea	1812
Manuel Lisa	1820
Jedediah Smith	1831
William Clark	1838
Kit Carson	1868
George Catlin	1872
Captain Jack	1873
Alfred Jacob Miller	1874
George Armstrong Custer	1876
James Butler Hickok	1876
Crazy Horse	1877
Texas Jack Omohundro	1880
Billy the Kid	1881
Jim Bridger	1881
Doc Holliday	1887
Phil Sheridan	1888
Ranald S. Mackenzie	1889
Sitting Bull	1889
George Crook	1890
John Charles Frémont	1890
W. T. Sherman	1891

John Wesley Hardin	1895
Calamity Jane	1903
Chief Joseph	1904
Red Cloud	1909
Geronimo	1909
F. Remington	1909
Quanah Parker	1911
William F. Cody	1917
Theodore Roosevelt	1919
Annie Oakley	1926
Charles Russell	1926
Doc Carver	1927
Charles Goodnight	1929
Wyatt Earp	1929
Bill Pickett	1932
Libbie Custer	1933
Will Rogers	1935
Gordon Lillie	1942
Nicholas Black Elk	1950

Bibliography

Black Elk, Nicholas. *Black Elk Speaks*. As told through John G. Neihardt (Flaming Rainbow). University of Nebraska, 1979.

Blackstone, Sarah. *The Business of Being Buffalo Bill: Selected Letters of William F. Cody*. New York, 1988.

———. *Buckskins, Bullets, and Business*. New York, 1986.

Blake, Hubert Cody. *Blake's Western Stories*. Brooklyn, 1929.

Bruce, Robert. *The Fighting Norths and Pawnee Scouts*. Lincoln, 1932.

Burke, J. M. *"Buffalo Bill" from Prairie to Palace*. Chicago, 1893.

Burke, John. *Buffalo Bill: The Noblest Whiteskin*. New York, 1973.

Cody, Louisa Frederici. *Memories of Buffalo Bill*. With Courtney Ryley Cooper. New York, 1919.

Cody, Wm. F. *The Life of Hon. William F. Cody, Known as Buffalo Bill, the Famous Hunter Scout and Guide. An Autobiography*. Foreword by Don Russell. University of Nebraska, 1973.

———. *Life and Adventures of Buffalo Bill*. New York, 1927.

———. *Letters from Buffalo Bill*. Billings, 1948.

Cooper, Courtney Ryley. *Annie Oakley*. Hurst and Blackett, n.d.

Foreman, Carolyn Thomas. *Indians Abroad*. University of Oklahoma, 1943.

Havighurst, Walter. *Annie Oakley of the Wild West*. Introduction by Christine Bold. University of Nebraska, 1954. Reprint, 1992.

Hedren, Paul. *First Scalp for Custer: The Skirmish at Warbonnet Creek*. University of Nebraska, 1980.

Hutton, Paul Andrew. *Phil Sheridan and His Army.* University of Nebraska, 1985.

Kasper, Shirl. *Annie Oakley.* University of Oklahoma, 1992.

Kasson, Joy S. *Buffalo Bill's Wild West: Celebrity, Memory, and Popular History.* New York, 2000.

Lamar, Howard R., ed. *The New Encyclopedia of the American West.* New Haven, 1998.

Leonard, Elizabeth Jane, and Julia Cody Goodman. *Buffalo Bill, King of the Old West.* Kissimmee, Florida, 1995.

Logan, Herschel. *Buckskin and Satin: The True Drama of Texas Jack (Omohundro) of the Old West and His Celebrated Wife, Mlle. Morlacchi, Premiere Danseuse, Originator of the Can-can in America.* Harrisburg, Pennsylvania, 1954.

Moses, L. G. *Wild West Shows and the Images of American Indians 1883–1933.* University of New Mexico, 1996.

Muller, Dan. *My Life with Buffalo Bill.* Chicago, 1948.

Riley, Glenda. *The Life and Legacy of Annie Oakley.* University of Oklahoma, 1994.

Rosa, Joseph G., and May Robin. *Buffalo Bill and His Wild West: A Pictorial Biography.* University of Kansas, 1989.

Russell, Don. *The Life and Legends of Buffalo Bill.* University of Oklahoma Press, 1960.

Slotkin, Richard. *Gunfighter Nation.* New York, 1992.

Swartwout, Annie Fern. *Missie: The Life and Times of Annie Oakley.* Blanchester, Ohio, 1947.

Wetmore, Helen Cody. *Last of the Great Scouts.* Harrisburg, Pennsylvania, n.d.

Yost, Nellie Snyder. *Buffalo Bill: His Family, Friends, Fame, Failures, and Fortunes.* Chicago, 1979.

Index

Photo Credits

Photos are reproduced courtesy of the following sources:
© Bettmann/CORBIS—8, 20.
The Buffalo Bill Museum and Grave, Lookout Mountain, Golden, Colorado—3, 10, 11, 19.
Culver Pictures—2, 4, 5, 9, 12, 17, 18, 21, 22, 23, 24, 25, 28, 29, 31.
Denver Public Library, Western History Collection—X-31676: 27; Z-2380: 1; D. F. Barry, B-201: 30; B-529: 13; and B-941: 6; Joseph Masters, X-33352: 16; C. G. Morledge, X-31346: 14; Nate Salsbury Collection, NS-67: 15; NS-116: 26; and NS-236: 32.
Garst Museum—7.